DEPARTMENT OF THE NAVY
Headquarters United States Marine Corps
Washington, DC 20380-0001

21 August 1992

FOREWORD

1. PURPOSE

Fleet Marine Force Reference Publication (FMFRP) 12-48, *On Winter Warfare*, is published to ensure the retention and dissemination of useful information which is not intended to become doctrine or to be published in Fleet Marine Force manuals. FMFRPs in the 12 series are a special category: reprints of historical works which are not available elsewhere.

2. SCOPE

This reference publication was written in March 1982 by George K. Swinzow as an independent research project by the U.S. Army Cold Regions Research and Engineering Laboratory. The manual is divided into two parts. The first part of the book gives an excellent history which details the background of conflicts fought in cold weather areas. The second is dedicated to procedures, techniques, and methodology of how military organization can cope with the cold weather environment. This reference publication is a good source for members of all ranks and services who desire to learn about operations in cold weather spots.

3. CERTIFICATION

Reviewed and approved this date.

BY DIRECTION OF THE COMMANDANT OF THE MARINE CORPS

A. C. ZINNI
Brigadier General, U.S. Marine Corps
Deputy Commanding General
Marine Corps Combat Development Command
Quantico, Virginia

DISTRIBUTION: 140 124800 00

CONTENTS

	Page
Preface	vii
Foreword	viii
Introduction	1

PART I: WINTER WARFARE THROUGH THE AGES 8

    First Appearances of Winter Warfare 9

    A Promising Start and a Decline 19

    The Many Uses of Winter 34

    A Slow Shift 48

    One Hundred Years 52

    Mass Armies in the First World War 59

    Classical Winter War 64

    The Last World War (?) 73

    The Subarctic 98

PART II: THE ART OF WINTER WARFARE 103

    Deciding Factors in Warfare 104

    Military Art in the Cold 113

    Some Military Properties of Snow 125

    On the Degree of Unpredictability 133

    Fundamental Sources of Modern Wisdom (?) 137

    Unconventional Operations 147

Closing 153

		Page
PART III	ILLUSTRATED...........................	158
Note on Illustrations............................		159

Figure		Facing Page:
1	Genghis Khan...........................	161
2	The Spread of the Mongols................	162
3	Warriors on Skis........................	163
4	A Cannon...............................	164
5	Gustav I Vasa, King of Sweden............	165
6	Gustavus II Adolphus of Sweden...........	166
7	The Winter Battle of Tuttlingen..........	167
8	Charles X Gustav of Sweden...............	168
9	Frederick the Great, King of Prussia.....	169
10	Napoleon Bonaparte......................	170
11	The Battlefield of Waterloo..............	171
12	Crossing the Balkans in the Russian-Turkish War...	172
13	Crossing the Shipka Pass.................	173
14	Finnish Military Skiers..................	174
15	Finnish Jaegers.........................	175
16	A Squad of Skiers.......................	176
17	An Ambush Position......................	177
18	Carl-Gustav baron Mannerheim, Marshal of Finland..	178
19	Stalin..................................	179
20	George Konstantinovich Zhukov, Marshal of the Soviet Union................	180

Figure		Facing Page
21	Preliminary German Plan for the Invasion of Russia	181
22	Plan Barbarossa	182
23	World War II: The Command of the German Forces	183
24	World War II: The Battle of Moscow	184
25	World War II: The Battle of Stalingrad	185
26	A Snow Shelter	186
27	Battlefield Locomotion	187
28	Digging-in	188
29	Trenches in Snow	189
30	Tank Traps in Snow	190
31	Preparing a Covered Trench	191
32	Snow Cover Distribution and Duration	192
33	Snow Cover Formation	193
34	Snow Penetration by Fragments	194

LITERATURE QUOTED 195

PREFACE

The mission of the U.S. Army Cold Regions Research and Engineering Laboratory is fundamental and applied research in snow, ice, frozen ground, and various aspects of cold regions science and technology. The laboratory also sponsors independent research on a wide variety of subjects suggested by individual researchers, reflecting individual concepts of need, desire, or inclination. The subjects of this research may not necessarily be within the framework of the current laboratory study program.

This discourse was prepared by Dr. George K. Swinzow as an independent research program sponsored by the laboratory. The author benefited from discussions with and suggestions by numerous friends and colleagues. Dr. William St. Lawrence, Dr. Ronald Liston, Mr. Albert Wuori and Colonel Alfred B. Devereaux gave generously of their time, and made valuable suggestions. Mrs. Donna Harp rescued the manuscript through skillful word processing.

A serious editorial effort by Mr. Stephen Bowen added logic, comprehension and consistency to the manuscript. His accomplishment is gratefully acknowledged.

The excellent photographs illustrating winter warfare skills and the portrait of Marshal Mannerheim were provided by the Finnish Attaché in Washington. The German town of Tuttlingen provided the historical material concerning a famous winter battle fought there.

There is no way to give credit to the many others who helped with illustration work, advice, and suggestions.

FOREWORD

Historical literature presents wars either as culminating conflict points in the otherwise smooth, peaceful flow of man's progress, or as dynamic cataclysms that propel him into new situations. To be sure, neither of these opposites is expressed directly, but one of them might be adopted as an intermittent position by the unsophisticated reader. The naiveté of such an outlook might be debated and rejected for a more sophisticated position.

A more direct and firm impression is formed by reading a specialized part of history — the history of war. Here it appears more clearly that wars are inevitable, recurring events. A most exciting observation that evolves from studying the history of war is the periodic repetition of errors by great leaders. It seems almost inevitable that such errors as dispersal of forces, stretched-out communications, poor timing, and lack of coordination are bound to recur throughout history. Why do great leaders refuse to learn from each other or from the past? Often the errors, for which many must pay in blood, increased effort, prolonged misery, or total defeat, could have been prevented fully or in part just by considering the actions of predecessors in similar situations.

One fatal error which recurs with regularity is unpreparedness for winter warfare. The changes in warfare technology that have evolved in the course of history have eliminated many previously essential things, but not the need for special winter warfare skills. For example, oldtime cavalry troops had to rest occasionally; they had to feed and take care of their horses (which did not have ignition keys). Now, mechanized combat vehicles are more efficient and deadly than any number of horsemen. But when cold weather strikes and snow accumulates on the ground, the marvelous, sophisticated combat vehicles become immobilized, or refuse, as is often said, to respond to ignition key action. Personnel casualties due to exposure, frostbite, and cold in general increase catastrophically. Sometimes more casualties are caused by the weather than by the enemy. If there had been only one such event in history it could be, with some effort, explained, if not excused. But we are ready to demonstrate that unpreparedness for winter warfare is a recurring phenomenon that can contribute to a spectacular defeat for one side and an easier than expected victory for the other.

Since there has been very little reflection on the role of winter warfare in military history writing, and since great errors have a tendency to reappear, there is a need to select and to present examples of winter campaigns and show the deciding role of winter warfare skills. The main purpose of this writing is to demonstrate the danger of ignoring the skills and preparation needed for effective winter warfare operations.

History is an expanded chronicle of outstanding events widened and interpreted by the historian. Any event, or chain of events, is interpreted from the viewpoint of the investigator. So-called "objective interpretations," "unbiased views" and "unbiased presentations" simply do not exist. Whenever someone judges a presentation unbiased, it means simply that the opinions of the author are cleverly hidden or correspond to the opinions of the reader. The examples described below constitute a series of military events. The subjectiveness and bias of this interpreter are as follows:

1. Great leaders are often incapable of learning from the past and make similar errors in similar situations.

2. The greatest wars always take place in areas with the densest and most advanced populations.

3. Wars, with time, lose their localized role and affect greater territories.

4. Major wars last longer than one season; that is the reason for the very important role of winter warfare in the past, present and future.

Since general and special military literature does not emphasize the role of winter warfare sufficiently, subjective point 4 is the main point stressed below. Furthermore, areas with large, advanced populations are also areas with more or less severe winter climates, so point 2 also indicates the importance of winter warfare skills. In addition, it unfortunately appears that a good measure of a country's winter warfare capability is the severity of the climate in the area where its supreme military headquarters are located. Whenever the headquarters are located in a mild or tropical climate, there will be no trace of capability for winter warfare.

The reader is invited to make his own objective judgment about bias point 1.

Unlike analytical writing, this inquiry is based on selected past events, outlined approximately chronologically as much as the subject permits. It cannot be called complete, but may hopefully be demonstrative enough. The illustrations do not depict the text; rather they present additional points and expand the content. The literature quoted is listed at the end of the paper.

Due to imposed limitations this work is not a historical treatise in the classical sense. It publicizes a badly neglected subject by making historical facts on that subject available, but does little more. To accomplish this, it was imperative that the discourse be divided into three parts. An attempt has been made to present the message in each part, and to have each part maintain a degree of independence from the others. This has resulted in some reiteration and redundancy. A reader not sufficiently convinced by one part may decide to examine another. Or even to explore all three!

The writer is prepared to discover, that is, to hear from any reader, that he is in error, heretical and fallacious. That is, inevitably, a by-product of authorship. More important: the ideas, opinions and notions are those of the "discourser" alone.

INTRODUCTION

A Limitation

To emphasize the purpose of this investigation certain concepts will be examined briefly. Others will be ignored completely, although this presents difficulties. We cannot examine forms of government, for example, as they unify and lead groups of people called nations, but we will have to mention how the leaders of some countries have been influenced by their forms of government, since the leaders are the ones who have made the major mistakes on the battlefield.

In order to eliminate the need to investigate the reasons for wars (the output of a major paper industry would not be sufficient for that subject), we need only to state that wars are initiated by aggressive leaders in order to unify their people, to plunder, to conduct slave raids, to occupy other people's territory (lebensraum), to expand their own power, etc. History lists an unbelievable number of reasons for hostility, for wars, beginning with the "Golden Fleece" of Greek mythology* and ending with the Second World War, which, according to historians, has a long list of bewildering reasons and attempts to justify it, picked according to the side one is on.

Undefinable Concepts

The terms "war," "peace," "strategy" and "tactics" are very often used, misused, and used out of context and without consistency of defini-

---

* It is curious that the Tadzhiks of Central Asia placed fresh sheep hides in small tributaries of the rivers Vakhsh and Zerafshan, kept them there during high water, then dried and burned them. The residue contained gold dust.

tion. It is remarkable that, lacking a consistent set of definitions, people still understand each other perfectly. Apparently, we are dealing with concepts often limited to suit the user's purpose. Von Clausewitz (1832), definitely an outstanding authority, defines war in a way that excludes revolutions, civil wars and military actions by groups of people other than governments. His thinking reveals the perpetual great weakness in the process of government's action. Clausewitz insists that governments must have complete control over the development and deployment of the military machineries available to them. And that is a great inner conflict in the government itself. Heads of government are experts in doing government work, in governing the people or the country. Yet those heads of government must have the power to determine the time and place of military action. Both the time of military action and the locality where it takes place are important elements of strategy, and strategy should be in the hands of generals. Clausewitz has a very clear conception of strategy, which begins with selecting of a proper time and place and ultimately ends with imposing one's will upon the adversary. Clausewitz also states that as a "continuation of political action by other means," a war must be started with a clear political purpose that extends beyond ultimate victory. The absence of such a clear purpose may prove more disastrous than a clear defeat in the field.

According to Clausewitz war begins with aggression. Aggressiveness may be the innate property of a nation. Characteristically (although not necessarily openly) the aggressiveness of a given government system must be documented in official philosophy. But it is always camouflaged in a demagogic form intended to create the appearance of the opposite. The terms "aggressiveness" and "peacefulness" are political jargon and therefore lose their meaning when used in political pronouncements. Also, both terms are relative. Absolute peacefulness becomes its dialectic opposite - it precipitates war. War is apparently a historical necessity characteristic of man (Vaida, 1976). "Perpetual peace" is a historically recurring phenomenon; it seems to appear between wars. Along the same line of thought one may say that peacetime is the time for war preparations, and intensive accumulation of war potential by a peaceful nation has the effect of postponing a war.

Since most modern political ethics teach that peace is good and war is cruel, inhuman and bad, eloquent statesmen, politicians and diplomats, subconsciously avoiding rude language, have introduced such nebulous terms as "armed conflict," "force interjection," "intervention," and "help in conflict," etc. Other terms are continually being invented for this purpose. None of these terms need special definitions and all of them mean the same - war. Therefore, in dealing with war we're dealing with unclear and muddled definitions. The same could be said about peace.

The Season, the Weather and the Climate

We have another difficulty with the concept "time of war." One may say that between the beginning of a war and its end is the time for fighting the war - is the actual war. That is imprecise and wrong. The Thirty-Years War actually comprised many battles and many years. The Hundred-Years War between England and France was not a long-lasting war, it was a 100-year period with many wars and battles. So we can simply say that a war may consist of one or more battles and may be short or long.

To simplify what we have to convey, we may say that a short war can begin and end within one season of the year - a summer or a winter. A long

war, which lasts longer than one season, requires some small or large
adjustments, changes and measures, indicating that time, or rather the
season, must be considered. Such a consideration may be termed "a strategic consideration." The role of winter in warfare is essentially the
subject of the present effort. The rest of the seasons are disregarded,
perhaps due to lack of interest by the author. We will for simplicity
recognize only two seasons - summer and winter. This book is concerned
with warfare in winter, a season with drastically different requirements
for survival and functioning. It might be defined, for the purpose of this
review, as a season with a clear predominance of below-freezing temperatures, freeze-up of open water bodies, formation of snow cover on the
ground, and shorter periods of daylight. The severity of these factors
changes with latitude and climate.

From the viewpoint of military science, cold regions are those where
troop and equipment movement is affected by snow and low temperature for at
least one month per year. Using this definition, at least one-half of the
world's dry land is in cold regions. Bates and Bilello (1966) gave a very
good definition of cold regions: those affected by classical wintertime.
Wintertime is an advantage to the army that is better trained and better
prepared for winter warfare. If both adversaries are equally strong,
equally equipped, and equally trained, the one with better winter warfare
capabilities has the advantage, and has a greater chance to win a decisive
battle. However, there are no absolute equalities in strength, quantity
and quality of equipment, or, especially, leadership skill. After all, the
side which begins a war usually believes itself to be superior, but very

often, especially in the case of winter warfare, that turns out to be an error.

A traditionally trained military force faces, with the onset of the winter, a series of new problems differing so drastically from those of other climates or seasons that it finds itself engaged in action that is far from traditional. The landscape, snow-covered and drifted over, requires different clothing for warmth and camouflage. Everything – shelters, machines, men – becomes visible in a different way than before, and new detection methods become effective and have to be counteracted. Ground movement of men and machines leaves visible tracks. In the cold, sophisticated firearms fail to function, and special cold-start techniques must be used on internal combustion engines. Deep snow may slow down or completely stop off-road fighting vehicles.

Besides special clothing, men in battle need more ammunition and more and better rations, but delivery has a tendency to slow down or even to stop. Behind the lines, roads must be kept free of snow, and at the battlefront swamps and rivers may become crossable. While most movement slows down or stops, ski troops, if properly trained and equipped, acquire a mobility similar to that of cavalry (we will show how readily that has been forgotten through the ages). But the fast skier also needs food and ammunition, and he needs a warm shelter at least once in a while. Frost injuries, especially among poorly trained troops, are a nightmare for medics, and many wounded soldiers who would ordinarily have a chance to survive and return to the battlefield become permanent casualties.

Perhaps the most serious incapacitating factor is low morale. In all wars and at all times there are a number of individuals who loiter in the rear without actual need or purpose. In the wintertime the number of men in the rear echelon increases dramatically, and it requires an energetic commander and established military "tradition and culture" to control the phenomenon. In very general terms it seems that the higher the ratio of support people (headquarters personnel, rear echelon, etc.) to people actually in the front lines, the lower the capability for winter warfare. Also, the higher the number of headquarters, command posts, battle stations and intermediate supply positions, the lower the winter warfare capability of a military organization. All these "elements" consist of men which must be fed, clothed, and sheltered. The irony of the situation centers on the fact that rear echelon people are better supplied with scarce essentials than the troops in the front lines. Often, the farther to the rear, the better supplied the personnel are. One example may illustrate this grotesque situation. During the Second World War the Germans developed a personal heat source, consisting of a package of chemicals that was activated by a cup of water. The gentle heat emitted lasted for several hours. It was intended to keep wounded soldiers warm during evacuation from the battlefield in winter. Numerous observers stated that most of these packages were used by clerks at various headquarters to sit on while serving their "combat duty." This may illustrate the situation to a sufficient degree.

All other conditions equal, the most important factors determining an army's winter warfare capability are the individual soldier's willingness to accept hardship, the quality of his training, including survival skills, and his morale. The Germans' claim, that the level of sophistication and the extent of so-called "civilization" were the deciding factors in superiority, was clearly proven wrong. Superior weapons and mobility and a lavish supply of technological amenities may offset the advantages of stamina, training and morale only to a certain point. We know by now only too well that whoever comes to the battlefield with superior weapons, but lacks training, motivation and morale, will soon find himself an unwilling materiel supplier to the enemy.

Training, morale and stamina are the factors that make a good winter warrior. Armies, good or bad, trained or untrained, may find themselves in winter trying to carry on a dragged-out campaign, unwillingly practicing winter warfare. In other cases, the wintertime might be deliberately selected for its advantages. Snow and low temperatures may be a disadvantage to the less trained, less disciplined or poorly motivated force. Then they become a strategic advantage to the trained, motivated combatant.

It seems logical to begin with a review of such cases.

PART I

WINTER WARFARE THROUGH THE AGES

FIRST APPEARANCES OF WINTER WARFARE

It appears that the development of winter warfare is a phenomenon that it is impossible to treat chronologically. It is also difficult to trace the development of winter warfare skills parallel to technological advances. It will become apparent that while new machines, weapons and tools have enhanced battlefield performance and resulted in irreversible tactical changes, some of the innovations eliminated, quite unexpectedly, the capability of conducting warfare in the winter.

Efforts to increase the ability to fight often seem to overshadow the need to clothe, feed and shelter an army. Also, the need for new weapons and war materiel leaves unattended the need to move and maneuver. Finally, the urge to create impressive masses of soldiers leaves the need for special training unmet. We will show that training, clothing, and equipment specially adapted for the winter constitute advantages if accompanied by proper tactical concepts. But there will be examples of grave errors resulting from simple lack of comprehension of the fact that winter changes the terrain drastically and gives the battlefield new properties.

Most unexpected are the numerous errors connected with winter warfare committed by leaders. It seems, also, that commanders are often unwilling to draw conclusions from errors committed in the past. We will try to point that out.

A chronological approach to winter warfare and campaigns in the winter should probably begin with the adventures of Xenophon (431-350 BC), or of Alexander the Great (356-323 BC), or of Hannibal (247-183 BC) for his glorious crossing of the Pyrenees and the Alps with elephants. But there is no evidence whatsoever that these great men made any special effort to employ winter strategically. Had winter any advantage for them? There is no trace of evidence of it. Did these men take any special measures to make their lives easier in the winter? This is also unknown; probably not. Historical works do not mention anything of that nature. Winter just came upon these people and they had to fight or march as readily as they did in the summer. Winter warfare can differ so substantially from military action in warmer seasons that, if practiced deliberately by using the conditions to advantage, it must be considered a separate military art requiring separate tactics. Here we must emphasize again that we are not considering cases where campaigns dragged on into the winter and both sides found themselves handicapped by low temperatures, snow, and ice. Such cases can be found throughout history and are usually of no special interest.

An outstanding case where winter was deliberately selected as an advantageous period of the year for a military operation was the early part of the westward thrust by the Mongolians. Genghis Khan* unified and ruled the Mongolians by leading them in a series of field campaigns which eventually resulted in Mongolian rule and domination of a sizable part of the European continent. The Mongolians were a nomadic people comprising

---

*Genghis (or Tshengis) Khan was born about 1162 and died in 1227; his true name was Tamugin of the Borgigin clan.

many independent pastoral tribes with a clan- or family-structured leadership and an undefined territory. Clan rivalry, competition for leadership, hostility and intrigue were the reasons why the Mongolians were not a serious threat but only a nuisance to their neighbors. Genghis Khan recognized that because of their cultural stage and their peculiar way of life, unifying the clans by force and intrigue was not the same as keeping them unified.

To interest them in staying unified, Genghis Khan led the Mongolian nation into many successful conquests in an ever-widening circle. In 1215 a part of China was subdued; the city of Peking was occupied. Then came Central Asia, the Khorezm Khanate as it was called then, which is now a part of Russia. And in 1241 the Mongolians invaded Hungary. In their campaigns the Mongolians invaded only loosely conglomerated city-states. Their purpose was not so much rule and organization as booty, plunder and taxation. Incidentally, unification against the Mongolians, as opposed to organization and unification by the Mongolians, was the reason for their subsequent decline. After the battle at Kulikovo Field in 1380, Mongolian rule began to decline. The Mongolians were a barbaric and illiterate group of people without any concept of orderly governing. Their main skill and their main capability and strength was martial art. Genghis Khan, as well as his grandson, Kublai Khan (1215-1294; called by his contemporaries "the wise Khan"), were superb, perhaps unsurpassed leaders of horse armies. Kublai Khan, incidentally, is very well known to the West through Marco Polo, the famous Italian traveler. He concentrated on Eastern and South Asiatic conquests and control, while Genghis Khan was the leader who developed innovative and progressive (for his time) cavalry combat methods. As we now well know, the use of massed horsemen presents numerous difficulties with forage, supplies, shelter, gear. Of all that, the Mongolians were masters. Also, leading masses of horsemen into battle, and conducting battles without the closed mounted formations that were invented much later, was an achievement revolutionary for the time. Later in history, Napoleon would have appreciated some of Genghis's skills (Howarth, 1876).

After unifying the Mongols in 1206 through a series of invasions and raids into China, Genghis Khan refined his tactics to perfection. He recognized what is now to a degree an axiomatic reality: the greatest expenditure of materiel, effort and time is not made on the battlefield, but in reaching it. He used to say that only life is expended on the battlefield, but great effort is expended in getting there. His masses of horsemen, traveling "on three horses" (each man had several spare horses with him), were able to cover up to 100 km (about 62 miles) a day. In those long marches they usually met unprepared and demoralized populations. The shaggy Mongolian horse, put to grass and rest at night, did not require special forage and was invariably fresh in the morning. While not very spectacular in appearance and only moderate in speed, they were capable of bringing masses of Mongolian horsemen over colossal distances, serving as relays and also as a protein source whenever the need arose. Slaughtering spare and injured horses for meat was an established procedure.

China, at the time we are talking of, was known to the Mongols very well. Information had been accumulated during the prolonged raids and invasions long before Genghis Khan's decision to subdue the country. There the idea of reconnoitering on horseback ripened. Individual scouts hardly ever provided sufficient information when they were sent out into the countryside. They were slow, and most of them never returned. Genghis Khan also never believed in evaluation by an individual scout, which was always subjective, sketchy, self serving, incomplete and often plain wrong. So for these reasons, he usually employed reconnaissance by force. At the peak of hostilities with China, he realized that soon he would conquer the country, and had to make plans for the future. At that time he realized that he actually had no information whatsoever about the nature of the land and people in the West, the direction of his next conquests and adventures.

Raids into what later became Russia began about 1210. The main purpose of these deep raids into the country was to collect information, and their most remarkable aspect was that they were always conducted in the winter. Bands of as many as 1500 horsemen assembled on well-rested, semi-wild horses from the best pastures. The men collected some very frugal provisions (hard cheeses, hard meat, some cereals and salt) and took off to the west. Each horseman led three or four spare horses, in the established way. The Mongols developed very efficient clothing, and mastered proper winter bivouac techniques and the right way to care for themselves and their horses. Fires were seldom made, and raw horsemeat was perfectly acceptable. Planning, timing and training, the three prerequisites of successful strategy, were excellent for the time, and suited not only the men and horses but also the geography.

The men traveled fast, switching horses frequently; they rested at night and easily covered close to 100 kilometers a day on flat land. Using wintertime to their full advantage, they always traveled along ridges, where the snow was shallower. Their horses could, without difficulty, obtain enough dry grass from under the snow. The bands, organized into units of tens, hundreds and thousands, were hardly ever detected by the sparse agricultural population of the area. The population was in villages, and the villages were in valleys. In the wintertime the people were huddled in their huts, and did not detect the passing Mongols in time to warn the remote cities. Robbing and burning of a few villages took place near their destinations, mainly to augment their frugal provisions for the way back. The population was alarmed but invariably too late. The disunited Slavic city-states were unable to provide meaningful resistance against the marauding Mongols. When they finally managed to muster organized resistance, it turned into a disaster. The Mongols appeared en masse and, operating in familiar territory, defeated the Slavic rulers everywhere they went. This was the way the Mongolian hold over Russia began.

The year 1223 is usually considered the beginning of Mongolian dominance over Russia (as Vladimirtsev mentioned). The Russians had lost a battle known as the Kalka River Defeat. However, the Mongolians did not invade the Russian heartland at this time; they returned to their pastures and left the Slavic tribes more or less alone for 12 years (Sergeevsky, 1954).

The Kalka Battle gave the Mongols, besides a victory, some good information about the tactics the Slavic leaders had been practicing. The winter raids continued to bring information about climate, waterways, obstacles and population centers. In 1236 the Mongols decimated the Volga Bulgars, who were a threat to their right flank. And in the winter of 1237 the Mongols appeared before the city of Riazan, the center of the loose association of city-states which began at the time to call itself Roosj (Russia). The statement of a contemporary chronicle about the Mongolian demand upon the Russian population is very interesting. The Mongols said, "Give us one-tenth of your rulers, one-tenth of your people, of your black horses, of your white horses, give us one-tenth of everything." That would presumably keep them satisfied. The Russians answered: "When nobody of us is alive, everything will be yours."

It happened exactly that way. The Mongolians moved in large masses. Marching on the ice of frozen waterways, they brought heavy siege machines and breached the walls of the city of Riazan within five days. As was the Mongolian custom with resisting centers and cities, the population was massacred. From Riazan, still using the river ice to transport their heavy machinery and siege supplies, and swiftly annihilating the two small fortified towns of Kolomna and Moscow, the Mongolians moved on and breached the fortress of Vladimir by 7 February 1238, and also annihilated its population. By March, 14 cities had been destroyed, and the uncoordinated resistance of the Slavs had become ineffectual. Then the Mongolians withdrew to their pastures. By 6 December 1240, after taking due notice of its beauty and architectural wonders, the Mongols burned and destroyed the city of Kiev. By 1242 Hungary was conquered.

The Mongolian hold over Russia lasted until 1480. The decline of their power began after the battle of Kulikovo Field (1380), but that decline was a gradual one. Their main achievement was the recognition of the winter as an advantageous season for campaigning against sparsely populated lands with clustered, sedate agricultural populations. In doing this they developed their mass cavalry tactics to a state of perfection for the time. Would they have succeeded in summer campaigns? Perhaps, but possibly at a higher cost in battle losses. The population, forewarned and alarmed, would have organized pockets of resistance in many places, and at best there would have been guerilla resistance, which the Mongolians didn't like and tried to avoid. Resupply of raiding parties would have been more difficult and the Mongolian horse would have been in poorer physical shape after the winter.

It is considered that the period of Mongolian domination was an important formative period in Russia. The growing desire for unity as opposed to feudalistic independence and the shift of the power center deeper into the Eastern European plain were important events in shaping Russian history (Kliuchevsky, 1904). Unlike in the previous greater conquest, that of China, the Mongolians were not very much interested in imposing a new government upon the Russian land. Perhaps they found the European population, as opposed to the Chinese, and the European ideology too different for their rudimentary conception of government. That may have been the reason why Kublai Khan went to great lengths to preserve and to support all the local rulers. All the Mongolians were interested in was tribute in goods, cattle and slaves. That was, perhaps, their only great weakness (Vladimirtsev, 1922). But the main thing is that the Mongolians discouraged local feuds and required peace in the conquered countries.

As a historical event, the Mongolian appearance may be of major significance, perhaps of even greater significance than the Romans in history.

After all, the Mongols controlled much more territory and affected many more people and material goods than the Romans ever did. Their winter warfare methods were most innovative. Is it fortunate that they were so thoroughly forgotten? Yes, fortunate for Russia. The Mongols actually forced the unification of Russia. But none of the subsequent invaders of the country learned from the Mongols. They came in the summer. Was the winter a surprise for them? Yes, it was a deadly surprise!

Much is known about the anthropologic difference between the races. Much nonsense has been written about the superiority and inferiority of various races, race purity, etc. The fact is that since a pre-historic period of isolated growth and "pure" race formation, all historical processes have been race-mixing. Wars, the business of killing people, have historically been tools of race-mixing. An example is the first occupation of Germanic land by the Romans. The Germanic population of southern Bavaria has a clearly Mediterranean look. Russians in many areas display a striking Finno-Mongolian appearance. Are there pure races?

What else have the Mongolians left behind? First of all, and most important, a unified Russia, a nation speaking several Slavic dialects, unified and with a powerful appetite for expansion. They have continued expanding for several centuries. But a discussion of that subject would lead us away from winter warfare. Except perhaps for the Russian's tendency to accept and use the harsh winter as a time to travel, to work in the forest; a time for intensive agricultural commerce.

Something else derived from the Mongolians: their horses. The large Slavic battle horse was replaced by the enduring Mongolian pony. The Cossacks would not have been the same without it. The horse, and better winter clothing. But most of all the new attitude toward the winter opened new opportunities. Siberia was ready to be colonized.

A PROMISING START AND A DECLINE

We have mentioned that battles prolonged into the winter, where both sides are handicapped by snow and cold weather, do not necessarily exemplify any mastery of winter warfare. To be sure, there are many examples of winter warfare, and with them many great leaders. We have already mentioned Xenophon, who was born in 431 BC in Attica and died in 350 BC in Athens, a very colorful personality of many talents. Xenophon had to fight battles in winter (Jacks, 1930).

Hannibal (born 247 BC, died by his own hand 183 BC) and Alexander the Great (356 BC - 323 BC) both fought in winter. But we cannot see that they made any attempt to use winter to advantage, nor can we detect any advantage of an unexpected nature that winter brought to them.

An important achievement in winter warfare occurred in western Europe roughly at the time of the Mongolian exploits: skis began to appear on the battlefield. Around AD 1200 the Norwegians were marching, patrolling and conducting combat on skis (Firsoff, 1943). Their speed, agility and mobility in places where men on foot became completely immobilized impressed every observer. Like the Mongolian cavalry, ski troops were able to arrive where they were not expected or before they were expected. And that constituted an undisputed, colossal advantage.

But the expected refinement of military ski tactics did not take place. Instead, martial art and military thinking turned away from winter warfare for a long period. Russia was under the Mongols, who knew what to do in summer as well as in winter. The European armies began to grow bigger, and in a gradual process developed tactics incompatible with winter.

Big crowds on the battlefield cause confusion. It becomes difficult to distinguish friend from foe. Battling the Mongols never presented difficulties - the racial difference signaled whom to hit, stab, spear or send an arrow at. But in Europe, the "racial brothers" easily became confused in the midst of a melee. Some relief was provided by the flag: gathering around the flag and defending it was most useful behavior on the battlefield. Canvases by many artists (batalists) were beautifully adorned with flags on the battlefield, often at the expense of the "action." Heroism connected with the flag was a steady embellishment of the corresponding literature. The flag was a coveted trophy, a symbol; but the flag became insufficient for directing men on the battlefield. An improvement was needed.

The great and initially inexpensive answer was the uniform. These mass-produced garments were identically tailored and colored. The problem of confusion on the battlefield was brilliantly solved: just attack and kill everybody who does not wear the familiar clothing! The other side did the same. Uniforms became traditional and symbolic and were preserved by the toy industry and tin soldier collectors for a long time. But the immediate result was a competition in fanciness and a complete loss of functionality in clothing. The time for fatigues was ripe, but they did not arrive until long after.

Along with the numerical growth of the armies came the need for more discipline. Tactics required intensive drilling and training, marching in step, closed, deep square formations with each move made to the sound of drums, bugle signals, and rarely, shouted orders. The appearance of firearms added another factor: a decrease in visibility due to black powder smoke. There was more need for discipline. The appearance of artillery had a predictable effect. Competition for a heavier shot resulted in heavier guns (and thicker gunpowder smoke). Could such armies be effective on a snow-covered battlefield? Definitely not. Uniforms did not protect the men against the elements. Artillery and trains became immobilized in the winter. Who could think of skis then?

The warfare that evolved gives the impression of being artificial, unnatural and strange to a contemporary observer. Colorfully dressed armies of men marched on foot and on horseback over long distances, dragging heavy trains and artillery with them. They maneuvered into positions opposite each other, usually on a plain called the "battlefield," overlooked by hills to be occupied by the commanders and staff. Upon command, given by signal or message, the armies started closing in, stopping intermittently to discharge volleys of arrows and, later on, bullets. They moved, reloaded, fired again, and then, still in rigid formation, engaged in hand-to-hand battle until one side was routed. The battles were incredibly bloody, and by modern standards enormously concentrated. Strategy was simple — each side hoped to subdue the other by having better trained (more obedient) or more numerous soldiers. Tactics were equally simple: there were rules to let the enemy fire the first volley, rules for engaging the artillery, rules for the cavalry thrust. A number of such battles constituted a war, and a war was often not finished by the end of the warm season. As incredible as it sounds now, the opposing armies disengaged when the weather became bad late in the season and began a process called "taking to winter quarters," which means they occupied villages and towns to wait out the cold season.

The rigid formations and parade ground precision of movement became an ingrained concept that lasted for centuries. The "winter quarters" mentality is still alive in certain military circles. We will have to deal more with "parade ground warfare," which is a consequence of inflexibility in military thinking. This inflexibility may be the reason why commanders of all times have had so much difficulty with guerilla warfare. Now, however, there is a need to describe an example of good winter warfare, while emphasizing that it constitutes an exceptional example, rather than a significant change in historical outlook.

The sedate approach to winter warfare was boldly interrupted by the Swedish king, Gustav I Vasa (1496-1560), who once again employed skis on the battlefield. Gustav Vasa understood very well the essential prerequisites for a successful winter campaign. At a time when other armies were indulging in hibernal winter torpor, he trained, prepared and hardened his troops for winter maneuvers and combat. He said that his ski troops could move 100 miles a day (Heidenstam, 1925). In 1521 he successfully fought Denmark, with his ski army displaying speed, endurance and quick decision on the battlefield. A classical campaign against Muscovy was fought in 1555-1557. The superior army of the Russian general Ivan Bibikov was skillfully out-maneuvered and then defeated. His early successful field campaigns earned him the Swedish crown and led to the recognition that mobility was superior to bulk force. And high mobility could be achieved only with skis at that time.

Gustavus II Adolphus (1594-1632) ruled Sweden from 1611 to 1632. He is often called the Thirty-Year-War king. His ideas of strategy, tactics, and especially winter warfare were revolutionary for his time (Fletcher, 1892). In the Thirty-Year War (1618-1648) he recognized that smaller tactical units have more flexibility, and that a flexible line as opposed to a square, rigid column is advantageous. This, together with wider strategic objectives and his whole fighting style, were completely new in Germany. His radical thinking on winter warfare was limited to surprisingly obvious (now), simple principles. The armies of that time, in competing for superior artillery firepower, were developing progressively heavier pieces. The result was serious difficulty in coordinating artillery action with infantry in movement and logistics. Instead of supporting infantry in action, artillery pieces were often engaged in bombarding enemy batteries and were in serious trouble when friendly infantry became unavailable to cover them. That was the way the rudiments of the "artillery duel," that ultimately pointless tactical engagement of all times, were created. Also, the heavy pieces of that time could not be transported over snow-covered terrain very easily. That was another reason for retiring to winter quarters. Gustavus Adolphus developed a light sled-drawn, mobile artillery which operated together with his foot soldiers and supported them, and was said to fire as fast as a musket could be loaded.

Gustavus completely rejected the idea of winter quarters and, in order to successfully operate, employed meaningful training and care for his soldiers. Properly trained, fed and clothed soldiers (And that constitutes innovation also!) went confidently into the field in winter and were always successful. While commanders of other armies required that their men, placed in ranks according to their size, be subject to senselessly harsh discipline while on duty, they did not enforce any discipline during free time. Hordes of camp followers of both sexes debauched and pillaged occupied villages and contributed to the low morale of the soldiers. Gustavus Adolphus's training was purposeful. He insisted on discipline and demanded meaningful behavior, and his army was of high caliber. For soldiers off duty he required decent behavior, clean living and soberness. Women, drunkenness and marauding were completely eliminated. The morale in his small units was high. This was especially true in the case of his elite ski units (Dodge, 1895).

Another factor was control of the troops. Whenever an army unit reaches a certain size it becomes very difficult to control on the battlefield without modern means of communication. Gustavus Adolphus kept his units small and mobile, and in this way controlled them much better in the field.

His most famous battle was also his last. He fell on 6 November, 1632, at Lützen, in a battle with Wallensten who, ironically, was at the time preparing to disperse to winter quarters.

A few years before the end of the Thirty-Year War a very interesting march and winter battle took place. Friedrich Shiller called the battle "the merry battle of Tuttlingen." Tuttlingen, also called by contemporary documents Dutlingen and Duttlingen, is a small town in southwest Germany on the banks of the river Danube. In the middle of November 1643, French forces under Guberiant had the intention of taking to winter quarters. The weather was bad and there had been several snowstorms; it was time to give the army a rest. True to the spirit of the times a marching army usually "foraged" the area through which it marched, and was accompanied by a wild, marauding band which devastated a wide zone around the slowly marching forces, stripping it of all provender. For this reason, it was decided not to winter in Rottweil where the French at that time were located, but to march to Tuttlingen which, according to a reconnaissance, was "fresh," meaning that the houses had not been burned and the population was well prepared for the winter. So Tuttlingen and the surrounding villages were occupied by the French force. As the southern side of the Danube Valley (the right side) is hilly and wooded, Count von Rantzaw, the French field commander, put out a screen of patrols on all roads leading to the south, where, somewhere behind the hills, lurked the Bavarian forces under von Hatzfield and Johann de Werth.

Meanwhile the Bavarians, amply familiar with the spirit of winter quarters, concluded that there was a chance for a successful attack and started to assemble their forces. In order to enhance their chances, they captured a few foraging patrols of French and cleverly let them know that they were moving to Bavaria for the winter. Then they allowed the captured men to slip away. After thus planting a false story for the enemy they started working out their march orders. Without campfires, baggage or heavy trains they marched on secondary trails through the hills toward Tuttlingen. During the march the difficult task of movement coordination was masterfully performed. There was a standing order to capture all enemy patrols, which was successfully done. An intense snowstorm permitted the Bavarians to approach very close to the enemy outposts, and at 3 O'clock in the afternoon a concentrated attack was mounted. The enemy artillery, too heavy to place within the city limits, was captured, and to the great surprise of the French, turned immediately against the city. The panicky enemy were either killed or captured or dispersed into the woods. Rich booty was taken. Guberiant, who had been wounded in a previous action, died. General von Rantzaw and an impressive list of officers, together with 6,000 "common laborers," were captured (Zeiller, 1643).

The old contemporary accounts of that event constitute somewhat difficult reading. The language, full of barbarisms and bizarre spelling, is in some places obscure. Certain works, however, written in Latin (Puffendorf, 1685: Historia Germanico-Sveviae), are authoritative and full of detail. The facts and names mentioned above coincide in several contemporary works. As near as can be told, the date of the battle was either the 13th or 24th of November 1643.

The Thirty-Year War ended in 1648 with the Peace of Westphalia.

Another Swedish king famous for ingenuity was Charles X Gustav (1622-1660). He was a statesman at the court of Christina of Sweden (1626-1684) and diligently studied the military art. When Christina stepped down he became King of Sweden (1654). A year later his skill as a warlord was put to the test in the First Northern War (1655-1660). In the winter of 1657-1658 he performed a remarkable sea crossing at the Little Belt. The sea ice was thin and the Danish forces felt safe, separated from Charles. By carefully testing the ice and reinforcing it by flooding a layer of planks and straw, which he allowed to refreeze, Charles crossed the Little Belt. It appears that his most important measure was carefully spreading out men, horses and baggage, thus avoiding load concentrations. The commander of one of his cavalry units, Count Bertelskiold, approached the problem in another manner. He apparently assumed that a short-duration load application would allow the ice to support a heavier load, and attempted to cross the ice with a closed column at full speed. The Count perished with his men and horses. Charles succeeded and won a tactical surprise over the Danes (Topelius, 1883).

In several subsequent marches Charles did not hesitate to use ice-covered water bodies in his military movements. The inevitable effect was always there. The adversary felt secure behind the thin ice barrier. The unexpected appearance of Charles produced the desired results (Heidenstam, 1925). What is thin ice for one may be just thick enough for another. Putting a purpose into discipline, taking care of the men to increase their stamina, and preventing "sinful behavior" to keep morale high allowed the leader to think about increased mobility, both in space (sudden crossing of ice barriers) and in time (winter warfare). The result was small, mobile units that solved the problems of maneuver and guidance, demonstrating innovation and pointing toward progress.

Perhaps with the end of the Thirty-Year War we begin to see that from the early 17th century on, the idea of winter warfare underwent a process of development and change. First, conceptual — no "winter quarters" — and then physical adaptation of weapons. When the going got hard, lighter weapons, lighter artillery, sledge-transported artillery, etc. began to appear on the battlefield. And most important, training and discipline became meaningful, flexibility developed, and proper care of men appeared. Actually, the advantage of crossing frozen water bodies had been recognized long before Charles. The Mongols crossed ice-covered lakes and rivers and used them for transportation. However, crossing a water body when the adversary thinks it is uncrossable, by reinforcing thin ice, indicates a very high degree of refinement in winter warfare technique for the time.

But the emotions of men with power over many other human beings led in other directions. A leader commanding ten units of 1,000 men each may win ten battles, some of them in the winter, against 15,000 enemies and feel satisfied. But commanding a mass of 15,000 men and engaging an adversary with, let's say, 14,000 men in one battle and winning it is a greater satisfaction! (This should preferably be done on a clear summer day on a suitable battlefield.) At the time of Charles and others, the satisfaction of viewing such a victorious battlefield constituted a much stronger argument for the traditional approach than any reasoning could provide. Thus developments moved in the pre-set direction. Generals needed spectacular victories and the battlefield needed to be spectacular during the battle. Therefore, men were sent in tight uniforms to exchange salvos of bullets, bayonet each other, etc. But men are naturally reluctant to be exposed and to die while killing others. The answer to that problem was training. Parade ground precision training, movement in step, absolute obedience to command, and automatic behavior were the only ways to control the great number of people and to mold them into an organized mass efficient in combat.

The strict discipline enforced by harsh punishment and endless training resulted in the capability of acting "as one man." Maneuvers on the battlefield were performed swiftly and precisely. Commanders had the ability to manipulate large masses of people molded together by discipline into square formations as "blocks" of people. The men literally fought and died shoulder to shoulder, instantly stepping over the bodies of their fallen and wounded comrades. The battles became so intense that blood shed by friend and foe covered the ground. It was the time of the bloodiest battles in history (although compared with the potential of future war they would appear almost harmless). Mass courage, stamina, and automatic execution of commands were the most important factors in tactics and the most important contributing to victory.

All the innovations that had appeared in the art of winter warfare up to and including Charles X were gradually forgotten and abandoned. The general officers, perched high on their hilltop command posts, needed more than ever before a clear picture of the position and movement of friend and foe. Therefore, colorful, "handsome" uniforms with decorative plumed helmets, etc. were developed. The soldiers, and even more their officers, looked more like pheasants (or perhaps we should say fighting cocks) than ever before. Since without too much thinking the idea that power is size and weight took firm hold with the developers, heavier artillery appeared on the battlefield once again. The functionally useless uniforms, the heavy trains, and especially the low mobility of the artillery made the return of the winter quarters idea just about inevitable. Forgotten was the battle of Tuttlingen. The development of the art of winter warfare came practically to a standstill.

The general trend of the times also affected those great developers of winter warfare skills — the proponents and beneficiaries of them — the Swedes. Charles XII of Sweden (1682-1718), during his campaign against Peter the Great of Russia (1672-1725), fought and won a battle with the Russians in Poland during the summer of 1708. But instead of consolidating his victory and securing his rear, he became drawn into a long field campaign which dragged into the winter of 1708-1709. Attempting to break into the south, Charles suffered from severe weather and began losing people to fatigue, freezing and vicious calvary rides. Supply trains and replacements were systematically captured by the Russians.

Peter's great achievement at this time consisted in the skill with which he extricated himself from the battlefield in Poland. He lost a battle, but not a decisive one. He skillfully kept using the winter situation, denying Charles a decisive battle until the Swedish army had become sufficiently weakened. Peter selected his own time and battlefield. At Poltava, in southern Russia, he fortified his field position in a manner which forced the attacking Swedes into dispersal and splitting of their forces. The results are very well known. The bulk of the Swedish army was captured, and Charles XII fled to Turkey (Topelius, 1884). The diminishing role of the Swedes in politics and as a military force was conspicuous in the European scene from that time on into the middle of the eighteenth century. These past masters of winter warfare began to abandon their position in Europe.

Generalship in that time was perhaps best represented by Frederick the Great of Prussia (1712-1786). This king, during the first part of his rule (he was crowned in 1740), engaged in a series of wars, including some winter episodes. In military doctrine he adhered to the principles set forth by his predecessor and father, and refined battlefield maneuvering to a parade ground precision never achieved before. Heavy training, exhausting exercise, strict discipline, speed in march, and quick decisions on the battlefield were his attributes. Intellectually refined and eloquent (in

French), he put many of his ideas down in writing. His unabashed view that the sacrifice of human life was fully justified if victory and territorial gain were achievable was apparently the key to his military thinking (Montross, 1944). In a fast field campaign with 40,000 men during the winter of 1740, he invaded, occupied and annexed Silesia (Schlesien). On the 10th of April, 1741, his Austrian adversary took a day's rest in the town of Mollwitz because of a very bad blizzard. Upon being informed of this, Frederick marched 9 miles through the storm and surprised and defeated the numerically superior Austrians.

Another winter campaign and battle took place at Kesseldorf in 1750. The Austrians occupied an elevated, fortified position. The approaches were steep and slippery with ice. Two Prussian attacks were easily repulsed by the Austrians. The third time the Austrians, sure of a victory, not only beat back the Prussian attack force but started a counterattack down from their fortified hill position and came within reach of the Prussian cavalry. Their retreat up the same slippery hill failed. Their ranks were broken. The Prussian victory was sweetened by the capture of 6,000 prisoners and numerous cannon (Carlyle, 1899). This was probably a rare, seldom-encountered situation.

Another well-known winter battle fought by Frederick the Great was the battle of Leutnen in 1757. The Austrians occupied well-fortified positions and enjoyed the feeling of secure winter quarters when Frederick, in a 250-mile forced winter march, arrived with a large amount of artillery together with heavy siege pieces, and began an immediate energetic attack. He employed a novel diagonal battle formation, reduced the Austrian fortifications, lost 5,000 men, but enjoyed a complete victory. This episode of the Seven-Year War was probably one of the most significant winter battles of that time.

During his 46-year rule, Frederick the Great did not contribute much to the art of winter warfare as such. The tactics employed in the victorious winter battles were equally useful in the summer. There was no difference. He looked to training for more effective firepower, discipline on the battlefield, and endurance. It is said that his soldiers were more afraid of their officers than of the enemy. The misery of snow, cold and darkness affected both sides. Whoever was capable of enduring more was at an advantage, and Frederick's people simply could take more hardship. Many investigators were much impressed by Frederick's strategic talents (Philipps, 1940). But there is virtually no evidence of special innovations or special strategic winter-adapted capabilities. Moreover, Frederick was not against using winter quarters to rest and restore his forces. He ignored them whenever he needed a victory or felt that his adversary needed the winter quarters more than he did. His greatest achievements were in iron discipline, improvisation, unexpected maneuver and the ability to overpower a numerically superior foe by attacking at a place and time where the foe could not deploy all his forces.

What we see toward the end of the 18th century in Europe appears actually to be a gradual abandonment of the idea that when the land is covered by a blanket of snow, the temperatures are low, and the days are short, another type of warfare must be fought. Populations became denser and conflicts more intensive. The warmth and comfort of winter quarters often had to be left behind. Battles began to be fought in the winter more frequently. The added hardship was countered by added training, discipline and drill. The armies grew bigger and distinct uniforms were still needed, even more than before. Proper clothing could not be used very well, and hygiene and sensible nutrition had not yet been discovered. Since men in the army were still a very small portion of the population, selection for size and strength was widespread. The artillery was heavy, but managed to follow the forces on roads and highways. The endless trains of baggage, to a great extent officers' belongings, struggled along in wintertime and often became separated from the main body of men. The inconvenience slowed down the armies significantly. Mass use of sleigh transportation did not occur to anybody.

THE MANY USES OF WINTER

People generally are born to be led; few are born to be leaders. A lucky gambler leads a flock of followers, admirers and imitators. When his luck runs out, he is abandoned, disregarded and forgotten.

A lucky, courageous historical personality, such as a warrior or king, attracts a flock of analysts, chronologers and historians. But when his luck runs out and he commits errors, resulting in lost campaigns and battles, he is not abandoned! His historians, chronologers and analysts stay with him, and by all means (concealing facts, inventing events, exaggerating and belittling) try to explain his bad luck in terms of an Act of God, circumstances beyond human control, and so forth. After all, the reputations of their leader and their country are at stake. Most of all, their own reputation suffers.

An example is Napoleon's 1812 campaign against Russia. Napoleon lost that war. But he won the seemingly decisive battle in the campaign. The Russians lost the battle but won the war. This was due to the fact that he made some grave errors, although the legend is that the "Russian winter" did it.

Toward the beginning of that period there were some changes in military art. There were some indications of progress. The great marshals of that era were able to move large armies at any time - winter or no winter. We would be unsuccessful in searching that period for new strategic, or especially tactical, principles in general, and winter warfare techniques in particular. To the contrary, whatever was invented was short-lived and soon abandoned.

It appears that this period is considered to have culminated in the beginning of a new era in history. One often reads about the Napoleonic time, even the Napoleonic Era. Whatever it may have been (time, period, era), our interest centers on the legend that the downfall of Napoleon (the end of the period, time or era) was brought about by winter and the winter warfare skills of his enemies, the Russians. How that legend came about is perhaps much less important than to attempt to see whether or not it was the truth.

Napoleon (1769-1821) was an enigmatic personality. His original name was Napoleon Buonaparte, later changed to Bonaparte. He was a Corsican of Italian descent, was well educated, and had a brilliant military career, specializing in artillery. Considered often the Ultimate Adventurer, he had the talent and reputation of a great military leader. At the age of 30, he became the military dictator of France. In 1804 he was pronounced "Emperor" of France. His experience was accumulated during long campaigns in Italy, Egypt, and other places (Dodge, 1904). His reputation as a strategic genius comes especially from such battles as the Battle of Austerlitz (December 1805), where he defeated the Austrian and Russian armies, or, for example, the Battle of Jena in 1806, where he defeated the Prussians. These battles have been studied and are textbook examples of Napoleon's successful military strategy, but they show no specifics or special measures useful in winter warfare.

The Napoleonic wars in Central Europe were fought to simplify "the political map" and impose Napoleon's will upon the continent. They displayed no special event of winter warfare interest with the exception that on the side of the Swedes and Englishmen there were about 2500 excellently trained and highly mobile Norwegian ski soldiers. They were highly successful at the Battle of Traugen (1808). Their success was typically due to mobility; they always appeared unexpectedly where not anticipated (Firsoff, 1943).

A large amount of literature exists on the personality, talent, leadership and capabilities of Napoleon. There are plays, motion pictures, fiction (most famous probably is <u>War and Peace</u> by Tolstoy), and factual historical literature. Fiction often contains interesting facts, and factual literature sometimes bears fictitious embellishments. There is no way to evaluate his personality without sharing the bias of the Napoleonic Legend, but doubtless he was a talented general and strong leader, attracting men who went enthusiastically to their deaths for him. Was he an especially good winter warfare leader? Definitely not. His exploits in Poland prior to his famous Moscow campaign demonstrate that amply. Napoleon ignored the advantages of winter and was often handicapped by snow and cold more than his adversaries were.

Studying the material on battles fought by Napoleon, one develops the impression that he gradually began to neglect to study his prospective theaters of operation. From what is known now, many of his battles were fought in partially unfamiliar territory. The impression is also that he either did not know or did not consider the events which brought about the defeat of Charles XII of Sweden. During the years prior to his Moscow campaign Napoleon slipped gradually into a remarkable "no choice position" which led him into a major war in the east without being able to resolve his conflict with England, so it was a war on two sides. After the battle of Trafalgar (1805) there was no hope of invading England in the immediate future. Recognizing this, Alexander I of Russia was in no mood to cooperate with Napoleon on his scheme for a "new Europe" and became openly hostile. Napoleon assembled his famous Grande Armée, consisting of 453,000 men accompanied by a colossal train and a huge amount of artillery. It was something that had never been seen before, and actually should have impressed Alexander without even a battle.

But Russia had space — space occupied by a sparse but hostile population ready to harm the invader in any possible way. This was something that Napoleon obviously was unfamiliar with. Whenever he had invaded or occupied a European country the population had continued to take care of everyday chores, placidly accepting another change at the remote top, a change they could not feel, but had experienced frequently before. Life under the new ruler had just continued as before.

In Russia the reaction to the Napoleonic invasion was different. The area had not been recently invaded by foreigners, and was unfamiliar with political changes since times unknown to the population. The natural reaction to the armed foreign invader, strange in behavior, dress and religion, was total hostility. Everything turned against Napoleon. Every soldier felt the "primordial" hatred of the population. Horses disappeared from night pastures, water wells were poisoned by carrion, tree tangles on forest roads appeared faster than they could be removed, soldiers could not move out of sight without the risk of perishing from a pitchfork thrust. Edgy, disturbed, and plainly frightened, the military masses kept moving where they were ordered. Morale suffered.

Napoleon crossed the Russian border in June 1812. Alexander did not react to this as expected. There were no signs observable that the Russians were preparing for a "decisive battle" on a battlefield. As a young officer of the Grande Armée wrote: "they evaded, retreated, and fled." The ponderous pursuit movement proceeded over so-called "scorched earth." Bridges were destroyed, villages were burned, fields were trampled, and resupply off the land was a dangerous, ineffective, almost impossible task. Foraging details seldom came back, and when they did they came empty-handed. Harassment by bands of peasants, night attacks by Cossacks, burned bridges and log obstacles in forests sapped the strength of the army, slowed it down, and undermined morale. Was this strategy adopted by the Russians correct? Did they actually have a choice? Most probably not. The army was in disarray and the commanders had been haggling among themselves; there had been no decision about a supreme commander. The forces were not consolidated and were practically unprepared. For this reason Napoleon moved almost unopposed, although very slowly, deeper into Russia. All he could do was to fight one or two undecisive battles and perhaps win them. Perhaps the most potentially dangerous situation developed gradually: the French forces were operating further and further away from their bases.

On 9 August, Alexander appointed Prince M.A. Kutuzov supreme commander, and Kutuzov rapidly assembled an army capable of conducting a major battle. An elderly, experienced soldier, a pupil of Suvorov, he had already been defeated once by the French at Austerlitz. Kutuzov had small hope of winning a decisive battle. Nevertheless, the famous battle of Borodino was fought on 7 September 1812. It was one of the fiercest battles in history. The Russians lost 60,000 men killed and wounded. The battle lasted all day, from sunrise to sunset, and fatigue on both sides eventually brought hostile action to a standstill. Kutuzov, realizing that he was losing his men, that continuation of the battle in the morning would bring either defeat or annihilation, and that the luck of battle would be on the side of the enemy, skillfully extricated his forces and abandoned the battlefield together with the capital of Russia — Moscow.

Legend tells us that Napoleon, assuming himself to be victorious, waited outside the abandoned capital for the "boyars" to bring him the keys to the city. But nothing of the kind happened. There was no indication of surrender or peace negotiations. What must Napoleon have felt at that time? The capital of a large country at his feet and nobody to pay tribute to him, no enemy army to contest his victory, or to surrender to him, problems with supply and control of territory, and a mass of dead soldiers to bury. Kutuzov's army had retreated to parts unknown to lick its wounds. Moscow had been abandoned by the authorities and by most of the population.

The rest is generally known from literature; it has been described many times. Napoleon's occupation of the burning city ended on 19 October. His great achievement, the long march through Russia followed by the Borodino battle and the occupation of the capital, had unexpectedly become a dangerous liability. Fires continuously breaking out in the city, the uncooperativeness of hostile remnants of the population, and drunkenness and looting by the troops had a catastrophic influence upon the Grande Armée's morale. Napoleon himself was badly influenced by the lack of any sign that the Tzar would be willing to negotiate with him. Nothing was proceeding right in any aspect of warfare. In preparing to leave the city the army loaded itself down with booty. Contact with the enemy force was completely lost. No small, light, mobile units were drawn up for peripheral security and no orderly movement plans were made. In this context the only two correct decisions, to abandon Moscow and not to use the devastated so-called Smolensk route on the way back, could not be implemented advantageously. Moscow should not have been occupied, or rather invaded, to begin with, so it was abandoned too late.

The French forces began the withdrawal from Moscow with a decision and an order, without any direct pressure from the adversary. In addition to all the errors committed before, such as not considering the extended communications, neglecting to consolidate the area under control, and occupying an otherwise useless city full of tempting booty, thereby triggering uncontrollable looting by men and officers with all its attendant demoralizing effects, new errors accumulated. The Grande Armée began its retreat without any contact with the enemy. The high command did not know where the enemy was or what its intentions and movements were.

But the isolation of the French was not so complete as it appeared to them. They were closely observed by the Russian command, and once their intention to break out in a southerly direction was reognized, the Russians decided to intercede. Marching south, the French forces would be in a fresh, undevastated area where foraging and resupply would present few problems. Skillful fast regrouping put the Russians in an advantageous position to prevent the southerly movement of the Grande Armée.

In the battle of Maloiaroslavets the Russians fought the French advance columns energetically and denied them passage. The French also found the stepped-up Cossack cavalry strikes (Platov) increasingly unbearable and were forced to take once again the devastated route used for their advance a few months before. Customarily this part of Napoleon's Russian campaign is referred to as the beginning of the great winter disaster. But it was not as simple as it may appear to have been. To begin with, the French army was tired, demoralized, weighted down with useless booty and to a degree disoriented. The French were also underprovisioned. The large provision magazines which fell into the hands of the French army were not requisitioned; they were looted by the soldiers, which means lost. The same thing happened on the way back in Smolensk. The supply magazines established with great difficulty for the retreating army were looted.

It appears that the French army was beaten by time, distance, and the lack of morale, skill and stamina displayed by most of the people, beginning with the lowest camp follower and ending, as we will see shortly, with Napoleon himself. We may say that the winter did not make much difference. Had there been no winter at all that year, a few more wretched people would have escaped and a few more Russians would have fallen. That would have been the only effect.

But we must continue with a few more highlights of that famous event. The well known disaster developed toward the bloody end: Marshal Ney covered the retreat of the French army with 12,000 men, but soon it became known that over half of them had no weapons. Most of the time Ney had no connection or contact with the main forces. At one point, he was cut off by Miloradovich, but refused surrender and with great difficulty broke out with only 800 men who marched around the Russians. By November, after the disastrous crossing of the Berezina River, the French army had lost most of its men. In the final accounting, only 10,000 fighting men and some 50,000 stragglers escaped Russia.

What were the reasons for the catastrophic winter retreat? Was it the severity of the winter? Was there some catastrophic misunderstanding of the time, distances, and landscape? Who is to blame for the disaster? It appears now that only one person, Napoleon, was the root and the reason for the carnage of almost 400,000 men. It appears that after assembling his Grande Armée he expected Alexander to step with his forces into his way and sacrifice the small Russian army before surrendering his country and throne to Napoleon. That was naive, to say the least. To pursue the Russians into the heart of their own counry, to expose their flanks to the Cossack sabers and the peasants' pitchforks, and to extend communications with the rear to the utmost were grave errors. It was an error not to evaluate time and distance. Was the onset of the Russian winter unexpected? Hardly. Was the winter unexpectedly severe? No.

Napoleon's 1812 campaign was known by the Russian people as the "twelve-language horde invasion." It may or may not have been exactly twelve nations, but there were soldiers from almost all Europe. This presented potentially serious problems with morale, discipline and loyalty. What was done to keep morale and discipline high? Practically nothing. Napoleon himself lost his nerve and fled ahead in a coach, and it is said that he was among the very first men to leave Russia. All his actions and decisions during that campaign indicate fairly cloudy thinking. It is also possible that his generalship was brilliant, dashing and great only in the familiar framework of the western European battlefields: first large columns marching into position on the battlefield; then, usually, an interesting evening session spent over maps; and then, early in the morning, colorfully uniformed formations marching out under orders from a command post overlooking the battlefield. With the exception of one real battle at Borodino all these satisfactions of great generalship were denied Napoleon in Russia. The fruits of a clear victory, as one might see it at the time, did not materialize. The occupation of the adversary's capital was only illusory. In any case, Russia's ancient capital, Moscow, was only a secondary focus of power — there was St. Petersburg (now Leningrad). But seeing the focal point of Eastern Orthodoxy — "Mother Moscow" — in the hands of the enemy did have a mobilizing effect on the population, and therefore worked against the French.

It is possible that Napoleon himself was the first to lose his nerve. Otherwise, how could all these errors have piled up on each other? It also would be a grave error to say that the Russian winter defeated Napoleon's forces. When the winter came, Napoleon had already been defeated. The winter only increased the number of men left behind. The winter did not make the life of the angry Russian peasant guerillas easier either. But the French had no winter training, equipment or experience. The Russians did not need training and had everything else. The Russian peasant could sleep all night long in a snowdrift and wake up somewhat rested and capable of continuing to fight and bother the retreating enemy. The French soldier, when forced to do that, did not wake up.

Instead of blaming the Russian winter for the catastrophic defeat of the French, we may point out that everything about Napoleon's Russian campaign was ill-conceived and unexpected by him. His great weakness was probably generated by a series of successes under predictable conditions.

Somehow, under the strange Russian conditions, he got out of touch with real events and gave commands while disregarding the actual situation. That may be in some way connected with the peculiar properties of a man who has absolute power over too many other men. It seems to be that in their minds, such men assume they have power not only over armies of men and life and death, but also over time, distance and nature itself.

What about the Russians? Did they employ any special winter warfare skills that made their victory over the French forces easier? The answer: none at all! But the campaign was complete with examples demonstrating the importance of timing, space management, and control over masses of people. The supreme leadership of the French forces had the goal of imposing its will upon the Russians. How could that be done? The only way they knew: march, prepare for battle, and engage the enemy on the battlefield. And they would win a decisive battle somewhere in Poland. Why did that not take place? The Russians knew that they were neither ready to fight nor capable of winning. Thus the big retreat. In the meantime the French moved into hostile space and gradually lost not only their manpower but their morale. It seems that the greatest error of the French leadership consisted in letting themselves get into a situation where they had to do something beyond their capabilities. They moved too far and too slowly, and lost what little control they had over the army. Meaningful centralized control becomes progressively difficult with increased size. A streamlined organization and new means of communications are needed after a certain size is achieved. That did not become available for a long time to come.

That the population of the territory the French marched through would resist and engage in a guerilla war did not occur to them. Closed, wooded areas are suitable for guerilla warfare both in summer and winter. But we have already pointed out that by the time winter warfare was developing the French were already incapable of meaningful resistance, and the role of winter in the great defeat of 1812 is an understandable fiction.

What is not understandable is the reason why nobody learned the lessons presented by the campaign of 1812. The need for flexibility in maneuvers was as badly felt subsequently as before. Artillery, with its propensity to bog down, was still the pride of commanders, and the flexibility, speed and endurance of Cossack horses was forgotten. Military thinking during the years after Napoleon was dominated by the works of Baron Henri Jomini (1779-1869), who thought it was a fallacy to chase the enemy; his territory must be occupied. His two principles, dominating the local focus and striking in the decisive direction, were well understood by higher military and political circles. At the implementation levels he was ignored. Typical is a reaction by the 1812 poet-warrior hero Denis Davydov; he said: "Jomini, Jomini... but how about a vodka ration" -- meaning that the daily requirements of the unit were more important than incomprehensible strategy. The result of the period was a disappointment: nothing was learned that should and could have been learned, and the rediscovery of winter warfare principles had still to come. The same type of battlefield confrontations between shoulder-to-shoulder columns of men occurred in summer and winter.

Russia had a special type of soldier, a serf conscripted into the army practically for a lifetime. Excellently trained, enduring, willing to undergo colossal hardships, this soldier had excellent morale; religiosity and patriotism were one and the same to him, and he conscientiously and devotedly obeyed the commands of his officers. An additional special feature was a notable variety of ages: among old, experienced veterans were young peasant boys who learned the fine points of battlefield survival from their older comrades.

The only real change in respect to winter warfare in Russia at that time was march norms and orders especially adapted for winter conditions, better uniforms and bivouac equipment, and, temporarily at least, less reliance upon artillery. All that was progress, but it was very little.

When Peter Wysotski started an insurrection in Poland in November 1830, it rapidly gathered momentum and encompassed the entire country. The Russians felt compelled to subdue it. So in January 1831 Russian forces moved into Poland. It was a pacification campaign which should have lasted 3 months at the most. But since both sides were equally skilled in winter maneuvers and the Poles avoided accumulating large forces in one place, the insurrection lasted well into the fall of the following year. The Russians demonstrated their ability to move, bivouac and rest in the field in any weather, including winter. Their resupply trains moved, often with cavalry detachment protection, with no difficulties at all.

The Polish patriots, recognizing that Russian forces controlled limited territory and could not be everywhere, developed an initially successful tactic of strike and evasion, avoiding direct confrontation. Both sides were equipped for, and capable of, winter operations. Winter was an advantage for both in that impassable areas were converted into good sleigh transportation routes. Although the Russians were operating in hostile territory, they had numerical superiority. The Poles were bidding for time: they hoped, based on previous encouragement, for help from the West. The outcome is known. Help never came.

The Polish insurgents demonstrated much courage, tactical skill and winter warfare capability. They had to lose due to numerical inferiority. Nothing else had to be blamed for their defeat. Besides, they did not have Napoleon's eloquent historians with their "Russian winter."

What would have happened if the Russians had considered themselves prepared to fight at the beginning of the 1812 campaign? They would probably have fought a major battle somewhere west of Smolensk. As it was, they had no choice but to use the proper strategy and the only sound tactics. For that we credit not the Russian leaders' wisdom, but their neglect to be prepared and their disunity at the top.

The mild 1812-1813 winter is a lame excuse for Napoleon. He was finished before its onset.

A SLOW SHIFT

In the 19th century the populations of the European countries grew, and they developed industries capable of producing material goods and economic power, thereby bringing increased prosperity to the ruling classes. The complexity of economic relations increased and, at the same time, the sense of security and political stability deteriorated. Governments, driven by the need to secure their political positions, felt the urge to divert ever larger portions of their resources to military power. It became unacceptable for a ruler to dip into his treasury and hire a few thousand skilled professionals for the purpose of imposing his will upon his neighbors. Technology and industry provided weapons and ever-increasing portions of the populations had to learn to use them.

Nations, large groups of people under common leadership with defined political interests, formed coalitions, signed open and secret treaties, violated them, and intrigued against each other at an ever-increasing rate and complexity. At the very bottom of the whole complex maze of double crosses and diplomatic relations was a strong but not very clearly expressed desire: the weaker ones tried to preserve what they had in terms of power and influence and the stronger ones tried to expand their power by imposing their will upon others. Whenever refined savagery and camouflaged rudeness failed to achieve the set goals by diplomatic aggression, armies of a new type — national armies — were called upon. War gradually became a very serious business. National armies supported by national wealth with improved weapons and ammunition influenced to a larger degree the life and economics of the involved countries.

The increased economic basis improved warfare technology and sharpened and intensified international conflicts (Engels, 1957). Conscription, feeding, clothing and supply of arms and ammunition proceeded on a large scale. The armies were considered to be capable of fighting longer and larger wars than before. Single battles were only episodes. When winter came, both sides were prepared in terms of more sensible clothing and shelter. Winter was a disadvantage equally unpleasant for both sides, so there was no reason to cease hostilities. But still the longing for "winter quarters" was perceptible. Studying campaigns of that period, such as the 1848-1849 Austro-Hungarian war or the Franco-Prussian war of 1870-1871, we cannot observe any special measures taken, or winter skills or advantages made use of. The wintertime was an additional hardship which the soldiers were commanded to bear in the name of their country and out of devotion to their rulers (von Hersetsky, 1909).

It appears then that, perhaps with the exception of the so-called Great Patriotic War of 1812, there was little winter warfare skill developed during most of the 19th century. Industrialization brought about bigger, better-equipped armies, but by no means were they ideally clothed for winter operation. Military skiing was, with the exception of the Norwegians, in steady decline and disfavor. Only toward the end of the century in 1883-1884 did a revival of special ski battalions begin to appear. It is remarkable that Russia was behind the others in military skiing. Only in 1890 were there a few small ski units that were said to be capable of marching 70 km a day for 10-20 days at a time. But they were abandoned for reasons unknown, probably budgetary, and nothing more was heard from them.

It goes without saying that moving, housing and supplying troops in the winter puts special demands on the logistician. As the Prussian campaign in France in 1870-1871 showed, no proper wintertime logistics had been developed. Despite railroad transportation, the relatively mild climate in the area, and an abundance of settlements in the theater of operations, the armies on both sides suffered from exposure and fatigue to a degree where units often were completely incapable of combat (von Hersetsky, 1909). The lack of progress in developing winter warfare skills and capabilities may be explained in part by the increase in war potential experienced by the European powers. During previous centuries, monarchs conscripted and supported armies that were numerically small compared with the population. But the second half of the 19th century was characterized by evolving mass armies drafted from the entire population. Training and drill requirements changed drastically. Emphasis shifted more toward new battlefield requirements. Parade ground training was needed, but only as a character-building measure, as a means for developing and maintaining discipline and obedience, the ability to understand, to take and to execute orders under all conditions. Somehow winter warfare training of the troops was overlooked, and the regular peacetime armies always conducted their training maneuvers in the middle of the summer, preferably after harvest time when the fields could be used without doing too much harm.

An exception was the establishment of small, specialized units capable of fighting in the mountains and operating on skis. Those units, trained intensively in mountaineering techniques, alpine skiing, and survival under winter conditions, were formidable specialists in winter warfare, and their only deficiency was in number. France and Germany had only a few battalions (the Chasseurs Alpins and Gebirgsjaeger). A larger but less intensively trained contingent of Tyrolean Mountaineers existed in Austria. Russia had no mountain troops whatsoever.

As a result of the previous developments, we see now that the large armies were better fed and clothed in the winter, but, for apparently geographical reasons, were poorly trained to survive and to stand the cold. On a large scale there was still no trace of regular winter warfare tactics. The specialized mountaineer troops were very few and were intended for use in special circumstances. Since most transportation relied on horses, rarely on the sparse railroads, the difficulties connected with movement on snow and ice were still uncontrollable.

Although the appearance of rudimentary specialization in winter warfare, such as mountain ski troop training, indicated some progress, there was no widespread recognition of the advantages of winter operation. Winter was still a season to be avoided.

ONE HUNDRED YEARS

On 31 January 1878, the nine-month war between Russia and Turkey ended with an armistice at Adrianople and the truce of St. Stephano. It had begun with a Russian war declaration and crossing of the Romanian border on 24 April 1877. The war was conducted in two theaters simultaneously. Turkey was attacked across the Danube River and the Balkan Mountains in a main thrust and, as a secondary objective, from Transcaucasia into Asiatic Turkey.

Somebody said that a war always has political-strategic origins and strategic-tactical implementations. (The use of double words here is apparently due to the undefinable nature of the words taken singly, and their enhanced sound of importance when used hyphenated.) Whatever the definitions may be, there was a reason for the war. But most interesting is the way that reason is explained, depending upon the side from which it is illuminated. It is also an illustration of the way historical events are interpreted, depending upon the time and position of the historian.

The situation in the Balkans at the time was as follows. The Balkan countries — Bulgaria, Romania, Serbia, Bosnia, Herzegovina — were under various degrees of Turkish dominance. Only Greece was a formally sovereign country. Shortly before the outbreak of the war there was a bloodily suppressed national insurrection in Bulgaria. But all the Balkan nationalities were resisting their Turkish rulers to a greater or lesser degree, actively supported by Russia. The underground revolutionary movement of the Christian population of the Balkan countries against their Moslem suppressors had many forms but their main stimulus was moral, monetary, and leadership support from Russia. In the Russian society sympathy for the "suffering Slavic brothers" was great and permeated all circles of the society, including the Imperial Court in St. Petersburg. This Pan-Slavic movement was welcomed by the political leaders of Russia, who hoped to satisfy certain expansionistic ambitions. As the matter stood, Russia had been fascinated with the unique value of the Bosporus Straits and Constantinople (Istanbul) for many centuries; the power that controlled them controlled the passage from the Black Sea to the Mediterranean Sea. Therefore, while the national emotional reason for a war with Turkey was the liberation of the suffering Christian brothers, the political need was to control the straits.

But others were watching the Dardanelles-Bosporus Straits also. The major European powers realized the potential value of the Black Sea for Russia if it controlled the exits. It would be an inner Russian sea and would shift the maritime role of Russia to the Mediterranean. Also, this was a time of intensive Russian expansion into Central Asia and the Caucasus. And India was close to Central Asia, as was Africa across the Mediterranean Sea. France and England were sympathetic with Turkey. Turkey imported its war materials from these countries, and had their diplomatic support. That is why Russia did not dare to occupy Constantinople. Russia had, as the result of the peace negotiation, to be content with an "independent" core region of Bulgaria and the Batumi-Kars territories in Transcaucasia. Some diplomatic finesses!

For us there is more interest in the shooting war which began in April 1877 than in all the subsequent diplomatic battles fought. For a start, it appears that it was poorly coordinated. All the insurrections took place shortly before the war rather than after it began. Nevertheless, the invading Russians found sympathy, support, and a sizable number of volunteers among the Balkan population. Most significant was the intelligence support provided by the local population. Every day Russian officers received detailed information about the movements and intentions of the Turkish armies at all levels, while the Russians often managed to keep their adversary completely uninformed about their own strategic movements. After occupying almost unopposed the north bank of the Danube River in Romania the Russian army crossed it at a place where only local resistance was mustered by the Turks. After establishing a bridgehead, the whole army managed to cross the river in less than two days. The main Turkish forces were up and down the river with only area security forces between. The Turkish Danube fleet was cut in two and was kept in check with minefields and steam launches brought in over land.

The march from the Romanian border, including the Danube crossing, lasted until the beginning of July. Then the march south and into the Balkan (Stara Planina) mountains began. The Turkish forces, unable to organize energetic resistance, had to retreat everywhere. Their plan was to let the enemy penetrate northern Bulgaria and occupy strong fortresses east and west from the main Russian thrust to the south. The Russians attempted to offset the plan and twice assaulted the fortified city of Pleven (Plevna), with great losses. Due to losses, extended communications, and dispersion of forces over that ever-widening semicircle, the Russian command decided to halt, consolidate, and bring in reinforcements.

The mountain passes in southern Bulgaria were considered strategic thresholds for further advance, and were ordered to be held at all costs. The defense of the Shipka pass against repeated bloody Turkish mass attacks which lasted into the winter is famous (see Military Historical Commission, 1913). The situation at the end of the year was as follows. The Turks had a series of fortresses to the rear of the Russians, threatening their flanks. The Russians had the Balkan passes under control, threatening Sofia and the Maritsa Valley, which constituted a strategic avenue toward Constantinople and the Black Sea Straits. The Russian "Shipka Sitting" — occupation of the passes — was a mixture of proper strategy and inept wintertime tactics. The Balkan fortified positions, built with a tremendous effort into rocky soils, were strong enough to be held against suicidal Turkish mass attacks. But snowstorms, low temperatures, and colossal snowdrifts constituted hardships and caused resupply irregularities. The army was poorly equipped, supplied and sheltered. Losses to fatal and crippling frost injury, typhus and exposure exceeded combat casualties.

The crossing of the Balkans took place at the end of December 1877. The movement began at the right flank (western passes) and proceeded toward the city of Sofia, with subsequent crossing threatening the right flank of the Turkish Army retreating east down the Maritsa Valley. It appears that the strategy was sound, economical and successful. In several cases maneuver substituted for insufficient advantage, and the campaign presented the opportunity to test and establish tactical methods never used before.

The traditional tactics of attacking in square formations of "blocks" or columns as were used in Napoleonic wars were no longer acceptable. The use of new firearms resulted in unacceptable losses. By 1870 all firearms had become rifled and breech-loaded. The Russian Berdana rifle fired 8 to 9 rounds a minute and carried aimed shots up to 1200 meters. Others performed similarly. The majority of the Turkish weapons were similar, except that the Turks had a small number of Winchester carbines that fired 15 rounds in 45 seconds. Both sides had a great variety of rifled artillery pieces with different performance characteristics.

The new fundamental tactical attack element was a row formation of extended skirmish lines that approached the enemy by leaps and bounds, supporting each other with rapid aimed fire. The use of depressions and obstacles for cover was (unbelievably to older officers) acceptable and encouraged. This was the way increased firepower was reacted to. Hand-to-hand combat and bayonet charges were ordered from a distance of 40 to 50 meters.

The new tactics were so revolutionary that many units were drilled and trained in the new art right in the theater of operations, often in plain view of the fortified enemy. The intensive training, and especially the instincts of the men, who were reluctant to expose themselves in tight crowds to enemy fire, led to a degree of mastery. The new assault tactics were used in winter against fortified positions as well as against the enemy in the field (Zaionchkovsky, 1893). While attacking in field skirmish lines was found acceptable in the winter, there was still no trace of any special wintertime combat methods. True, the people, on the Russian side at least, were dressed somewhat more sensibly than Napoleon's Grande

Armée had been, but they were still not warm and comfortable enough. There was no sign of the idea of using white camouflage. The soldiers were poorly fed. War correspondents also made observations that the old-time soldiers' concept of tough and harsh treatment was still alive and resulted in a certain amount of unnecessary hardship (Nemirovich-Danchenko, 1879).

The political outcome of the war, ended at Sanct Stephano (Eshilkee on contemporary Turkish maps) in the spring of 1878 and agreed upon at the June conference in Berlin the same year, was definitely short of the initial Russian expectations and intents. As mentioned, only half of Bulgaria had a degree of autonomy. But it was a first step toward modernization in the Balkans. The colonialistic-feudalistic power of Turkey in Europe disappeared. The war was most important as an example of new technology forcing new tactics and new tactics leading to modification of winter warfare strategy. The rapid, precise fire of the Turks required attack in open formation and a new battle order. The great winter offensive across the Balkan mountains would not have been possible in columns such as were employed at the battle south of Moscow against the French 65 years before. The Russians would not have been able to bring in and place enough people. Since creative people and nations never forget new weapons and never return to older, less efficient ones, the new tactics on the battlefield could not be forsaken, despite the fact that the older, higher ranking generals never felt comfortable with them. Subsequent winter wars were fought in a new way.

The primitive errors of a hundred years before were not so readily repeated. White camouflage was invented and in some cases used. But we will see the same inability to learn from the past. The need for protective clothing, shelter and special food was often neglected. The need for special training, tactics and strategy would, in the hundred years since the Balkan engagement in the snow, often be disregarded. Why is it that past experience in winter warfare is not considered for the future? We will be unable to answer that.

MASS ARMIES IN THE FIRST WORLD WAR

The growing populations of the world, with their growing mobilization potential, did not produce any special new thinking about the need for a winter defense capability. More or less proper field clothing was adopted for all seasons, but otherwise cold weather problems were solved whenever they arrived, on a makeshift basis. To be sure, some of the improvisations were brilliant and functioned very well, but there were instances of utmost helplessness in the winter.

During the first winter of World War I, ski mountaineers demonstrated their ability to deliver swift and effective blows. The Germans found that in order to control the aggressive French Chasseurs their Bavarian skiers had to be employed. Regular ski battles were fought and there were indications that an interesting new tactic, based on the high mobility of ski troops, was in the making. Some talented leaders recognized the advantages of unexpected strikes and evasions, and swift retreats to avoid retaliation, especially by heavy weapons. The winter of 1914-1915 was unusually snowy in the Vosges Mountains. The excellently trained Chasseurs actually excavated fighting trenches in snow, and used white clothing for camouflage. The French Vosges positions were in some places literally snow fortifications (Ward, 1917). A seemingly promising start.

These promising tendencies in winter tactics, however, went largely unnoticed. The notion that success is territory taken and controlled was still firmly ingrained. Also, it was difficult to visualize the specifics of winter warfare from well-heated supreme headquarters.

With the few exceptions mentioned, all parties involved in First World War winter battle displayed very few special winter warfare skills. When the Germans attacked Verdun in February 1915, they attacked in broad daylight over snow-covered fields, presenting excellent dark targets to the defending French. The carnage of Verdun, as it was called in the press at that time, is further evidence of the fact that the idea of employing different warfare methods in the winter than the ordinary attacks learned and practiced in summer maneuvers was simply not thought of at this time. A night attack by troops dressed in white camouflage clothing might have been more effective. On the eastern front the Germans conducted several unsuccessful attacks on the Russian positions with a major snowstorm blowing into their faces. In the Carpathian Mountains Russian forces that had no mountain training and no ski troops at all were under continuous pressure from small Austrian ski patrols. It is not entirely comprehensible why the Russian armed forces did not develop strong, sufficiently trained ski units. They had the terrain, the climate and the type of men suitable for skiing. A general view of the events of the First World War shows that besides the innovative utilization of the almost 4-meter-deep snowdrifts by the French in the Vosges there was very little imaginative use of the winter. Essentially, all sides involved had to cope with the weather, and trench warfare with quiescent periods during bad weather (which indicates the persistence of the old "winter quarters" viewpoint) was the rule (Ward, 1917).

After the various armistices were signed peace did not come to all nations. A civil war broke out in Russia which lasted until 1922. The intensity of fighting did not appear to diminish in winter; large scale troop movements and maneuvering went on, using horse-drawn sleds. What is remarkable is that skis suddenly appeared on the battlefield during the Russian Civil War (Sokolov-Strakhov, 1927). America gained some winter warfare experience when a small expeditionary force was briefly exposed to the rigors of winter warfare in far eastern Russia. It was a generally limited action, but our troops had a taste of cold weather warfare. The Russians were excellently equipped and fought on skis. The Americans complained about very poor equipment, poor walking boots, etc. (Moore, 1920). The Russian participants were generally amused by the Americans' helplessness, inability to protect themselves against the elements, and unsuitable clothing and equipment. In any case we could surmise that the difficulties that were revealed by the experience which the U.S. troops had during that brief interlude were duly recorded and conclusions drawn.

It appears that after the Civil War the Russian military researcher's thinking was completely free of the "winter quarters" syndrome and they proceeded with ski training and investigation into winter warfare. Gavrichkov (1929) investigated ski marches and military skiing in general. He found that a ski soldier with a full pack could cover an average distance of about 35 km in eight hours of trailblazing, the maximum being 50 km.

Russian military skiing broke away from western concepts entirely at this time and went its separate and fully individual way. The western skiers, especially the German Gebirgsjaeger, well developed by the mid-thirties, trained on downhill type skis, which are very difficult to use in deep, fluffy snow and require sophisticated bindings with boots good only to approximately -15° to -17°C (0°F). But the Russians were accumulating experience with skis capable of supporting combat-loaded men. Trials were concentrated on long marches that lasted for weeks at a time made by self-sufficient small units. The rather modest range of fighting men on skis doubled, reaching 100 km a day, and much experience was accumulated on bivouacking, shelter, concealment and casualty evacuation. Together with it there was an interest in winter terrain fortification (Karatun, 1940).

It must be emphasized that the knowledge obtained at that time, although valid, good and useful, was by no means adapted by the country's armed forces as a whole. As is so often true, research, development and production (in this case incorporation of new items into the military system) always require considerable time.

Machines, weapons, transportation — anything mechanical — either perform less efficiently or, as is too often the case, do not perform at all in severe weather. Winter exercises in Russia resulted in established tactical procedures for armor (Knizhnikov, 1937; Amosov, 1935). Training manuals for all mechanized equipment adopted improvisations, resulting in relatively high performance during a severe winter. Also, the Russian tanks, with high clearance and low footprint pressure, were superbly adapted to combat in deep snow. As a parallel development, the infantry learned to throw up effective tank barriers using plain snow (M.K., 1938). The military press of that time reported achievements in successful winter maneuvers.

We may add, also, that Russia, by its climatic and geographic setting, was naturally expected to develop an army of skilled men capable of conducting successful winter campaigns.

CLASSICAL WINTER WAR

To engage in war, a power evaluates its chances for victory by comparing army strength, weapons, materiel, mobility, resources, skill, and patriotism, in other words willingness to fight.

A follower of political and military Russian literature of the late 1930's might rightfully have concluded that progress in the military art was being made. Never before had Russian military strength been as high as at that time. It appeared, then, that Russia could with very little risk and cost afford the luxury of pressuring its neighbors for advantages. It appears at the surface that not much effort or large-scale mobilization were needed. Nevertheless, commanders, to properly engage in a field campaign, must not only evaluate the potential adversary, but must be able to answer questions about their own state of preparedness. They must compare terrain specifics with equipment, and know the availability of materiel, the effects of propaganda upon the adversary, and the spirt, skill and knowledge of their soldiers.

A military conflict between Finland and Russia was ripening in 1939. It is hard to say how much true information the Russian command had about Finland's general state of preparedness for defense. Clearly, they had figures to compare. The Russian command could also compare quantitative and qualitative data on weapons, equipment and resources. What must have been greatly underestimated was skill, patriotism and morale. One pays for errors of underestimation, especially in a winter campaign. The Russo-Finnish war was for Russia a payment in blood. In any event, the Russo-Finnish winter war is a classic case of a defensive winter campaign. The winter war, as it was usually called, began in 1939 following a breakdown in Russian-Finnish territorial negotiations. Russia, having increased its Baltic coastal territory considerably by incorporating into the USSR the republics of Lithuania, Latvia and Estonia, wanted to "increase Leningrad's security" as it was put at that time by obtaining part of the Finnish shoreline, including the city of Viipuri, also called Vyborg. Finland disagreed, and on 30 November 1939 Russian forces crossed the Finnish border.

From the very first days of the campaign there seemed to be an unexplainable twist in the thinking of the Russian leadership. Armor was sent across the border where there was no suitable terrain, and in the not-so-frequent places where there was good tank country infantry stomped resolutely forward. Poorly outlined objectives and massing of columns along the few roads ideally suited the defensive doctrine of the Finns. The excellently trained Finnish ski units operated in small, independent, highly mobile groups off the road, avoiding enemy counter-fire, while the Russian columns, afraid of the forest, hugged the highways and huddled together seeking the security of open space (Suomailainen, 1949). Attempts by the Russian forces to establish flank protection were energetically counteracted. The commanders soon realized that to send out detachments to the left, to the right, or ahead meant to lose them as soon as they entered the forest.

In early December 1939, a Russian division marched west from the vicinity of Ukhta and crossed the border with the intention of cutting Finland in half. Their objective was to march southwest along the shore of Lake Kuotajarvi, then at the Oulujoki River to proceed along the railroad to the bay of Bootia. There was no frontal resistance whatsoever when the division (the 163rd) crossed the border, but soon after there were numerous ambushes from left and right. Flank protection detachments were useless and were lost. The division slowed down and the columns stretched out to more than 12 km along the main highway. The harassing ski patrols never attacked armor and heavy artillery. Instead, they concentrated on infantry, supply trains and, at a later stage, field kitchens and bakeries.

At Suomussalmi the entire division lost all communications with the rear, slowed down to a crawl, and finally stopped. At that time harassment picked up in intensity. The Russians attempted to retaliate with intensive artillery and mortar area bombardment. But most of the time the fire was layed down in empty space. The long column was broken up into five separate encirclements which suffered from shortages of rations, fuel and ammunition. A desperate request for help was sent out. A 24,000-man relief division marched west as fast as it could to salvage whatever was possible, but by the time it got to the general area, the 163rd infantry division no longer existed save for a few wretched stragglers who lay dying in the snowy forests and in Finnish hands from exposure and frost injuries. The relief division, initially more numerous than the 163rd, went the same way. Slowed down, stretched out along its route, losing men to ambushes, wasting time working around aritifical obstacles, it lost connection with the rear. The division was doomed. The Finns managed to cut it up into several sections and stopped it. Armor and artillery with its flat trajectory were ineffectual. From survivors it was learned that the personnel were conscripts from open southern plains who, unfamiliar with the northern forests, were paralyzed by fear and were dying from exposure, frostbite and sniper fire.

The most deadly effect came from the swift Finnish skiers, equipped with excellent Suomi submachine guns and hand grenades. They appeared in the most unexpected places and were swift and deadly. Characteristically a Finnish assault would last less than a minute, after which the white-clad Finns would disappear. In the night the Finns attacked heated tents by sneaking around sentries, ripping slits in the fabric with their knives, and dropping grenades inside. Bonfires, badly needed in the severe cold, were favorite submachine gun targets. The harassed, stretched, cut-off division, with badly depleted supplies, lost its field kitchens and was cut up into small pockets and annihilated. By 7 January 1940 it was all over. Two divisions had been annihilated, and 43 tanks, 10 armored personnel carriers, 1 airplane and large amounts of supplies had fallen into the hands of the Finns.

The double battle of Suomussalmi represented the favorite tactics of both sides. The Russians relied on massing men, materiel and heavy weapons. They were untrained for forest warfare and were not equipped for the winter. The nearest they came to winter warfare was when a Siberian ski brigade was finally deployed. These men were properly trained for ski mobility and were warmly dressed. But due to the absence of white camouflage gear and failure to protect their flanks, the brigade was trapped and wiped out on a frozen lake.

The Finnish tactics, based on a defensive strategy, consisted essentially of a flexible offense. They never directly resisted the advance columns of the invasion force. Guided by people who knew the local topography, using the terrain to their advantage, they attacked swiftly with deadly automatic fire, directing it at marching columns and vehicles. Slowing the enemy down, weakening them psychologically and physically, and cutting them up and isolating them in pockets was developed into a most effective art (Anonymous, 1950). These were the famous "Motti" tactics, which proved themselves time and again against the 300,000-man invading force. Col. Jarrinen (1949) gives a lucid description of the defensive doctrine, offensive tactics, use of skis and mobility. (For a review of Jarvinen's thinking see also Meyerhofer, 1949.) Up to the very end of the Finnish war, Finnish operations north of the Karelian Isthmus were distinguished by skill, valor, sacrifice and courage. There is no doubt that for a long time to come that episode will remain a classic of winter warfare and coordinated operation of small units.

As the Russians discovered during their slow, tortoise-like advance across the Karelian Isthmus, there was a strong line of fortification shielding Viipuri (Vyborg) — the so-called Mannerheim Line (named for Marshal of Finland C.G. Mannerheim, 1867-1951), head of state and Supreme Commander of the Armed Forces. This fortification belt, superbly designed and constructed, consisted of a network of interconnected, camouflaged bunkers, strong points and fortified positions.* With overwhelmingly

---

* There was also a viewpoint often expressed at that time that the Mannerheim Line had not been completed and was more of a symbolic deterrent than a serious tactical obstacle. But the fact is that all defense installations are either under construction and in the process of improvement or they are obsolete.

superior forces the Russians, suffering casualties from enemy action, frostbite and exposure, had to pinpoint the camouflaged bunkers and reduce them one by one, often actually excavating them with artillery fire.

But the inevitable happened — the Mannerheim Line was breached and the Russian forces could not be stopped before Helsinki. A peace was signed in early March 1940 (Mannerheim, 1952) but did not last long for the courageous Finnish nation. In June 1941 they marched at the side of the Germans against Russia. Had it not been for the territorial losses so painfully felt by the Finns, they probably would have been neutral along with the Swedes. Their aim in 1941 was the recovery of lost territory. As is known, peace did not come to Finland until September 1944, after tragic loss of life and land.

What actually happened during the 1939-1940 winter war? Why, with a colossal superiority in men and materiel, did the Russians suffer such losses and find themselves so helpless in the field? It appears in retrospect that the Russian high command did do just about everything wrong that they possibly could. They underestimated the enlightened, meaningful training, health, patriotism and skill of the Finnish army. Most important, they could not comprehend the strong national will of the Finns to defend themselves. In their hasty planning they assigned large amounts of useless artillery to positions in the Finnish forests. Their maps were poor and their troops were poorly equipped for winter warfare. The Russians knew about the Mannerheim Line and about the training of the mobile ski units. But the fact is that they led untrained troops into a winter theater of operations, weighted them down with tanks and artillery, and failed to provide them with proper clothing, including whites. All this, together with the inability to predict the outcome of engagements between ponderous divisions and small mobile units, as in the action at Kuotajarvi Lake, indicates only one thing - a complete lack of capability at the very top levels of military leadership.

And so it was. Russia had suffered the loss of 15,000 officers in the purges of 1937-1938, among them M.N. Tukhachevski, Bliukher, Govorov, Rokkosovski, all famous names and great thinkers in Russian strategic development, and many others. After the Finns rejected their territorial demands and Russia decided to march, there were very few leaders left capable of evaluating the prospective adversary, of training and selecting the manpower, and of arriving at a set of tactical options suitable for the time of the year and the terrain.

The outcome of the Finnish winter war influenced the evaluation of Russia as a military power. It was universally believed that Russia had a low potential for engaging in a serious war. Indeed, the results of this small winter war were really tragic for Russia. The USSR lost 48,000 men killed and 158,000 men wounded (mainly by frost). That was according to Russian sources. The Finns evaluated the Russian losses as being significantly higher. The annihilation of the two divisions at Suomussalmi alone indicates losses significantly higher than the official Russian statements led the people to believe. Official commentaries and the press were, as always, enigmatic. At that time (January 1940) schools, hospitals and student dormitories deep in the hinterland were filled with wounded and for the most part severely frostbitten soldiers. In addition to observations, to rumors, which always proliferate when official sources fail to provide information, there were the stories by survivors. Word of mouth goes a long way where public information sources fail to do their job. The public impression was that something terribly wrong had happened to Russian national defense, and, unofficially, public pessimism was deep, with a disenchanted mood prevailing.

The intensive official political propaganda of this time became ineffectual. Statements about the defensive might of the Fatherland, spread by Voroshilov, Budenny and Stalin himself, had an annoying and irritating effect. Due to a gap between the official statements and the observable facts the credibility of the propaganda reached another low.

Below the surface a feverish reorganization of the Russian armed forces and the armament industry began. Analysis, comments and evaluations of Russia as a military power that appeared in Western Europe were controversial. Sympathy for Finland was universally high.

While the public opinion of the free world unanimously castigated the deplorable aggression against Finland, there was no clear opinion about the poor military performance of the Russian army. The puzzle remained unexplained until Nikita Khrushchev partially lifted the curtain of secrecy at the 22nd Party Congress. He made a statement to the effect that Stalin's purges had encompassed military circles and that innocent higher officers had been victims; thus was explained the ineptitude at the very top of the army. But what had triggered the purges of the army? Alexandrov (1964) presents a fascinating story: the Germans, observing the purge atmosphere in Russia, skillfully forged documents implicating Marshal Tukhachevsky and others in high treason. The documents were imaginatively slipped to the Czech government (a German attaché had too much to drink and left a briefcase with the documents in a restaurant in Prague) and were presented by the friendly Czechs to Russia. The provocation apparently worked very well.

Whatever the actual origin of the purges was, thier consequences were felt not only in the course of the winter war but in the initial period of the Russian war with the Germans. Describing the state of the Russian armed forces, observers called a "Decapitated Army."

THE LAST WORLD WAR (?)

Russia achieved its territorial objectives in its winter war against Finland. It came out of it victorious and disgraced. In view of what will be discussed below, the losses in manpower must not have disturbed the high command. But the errors made did disturb them, and there were signs of a "mini-purge" in military circles. Curiously, the Russian economy was not affected very much this time. Signs of "normal" civilian life prevailed. Whatever the foreign evaluators made out of the Russian performance in Finland, the main display was ineptitude at the very top. Apparently it was a lesson for the Russian high command and the time was ripe for some changes.

Signs of change, at least signs of disturbances and perturbations, began to appear in military circles. Sloganeering articles of the aggressive Voroshilov doctrine type on offensive war in enemy territory began to disappear from the press. The Political Commissars in the army were abolished. There were indications of disarray at the top and a complete absence of clear doctrine and confident leadership. It was evident that the high command lacked the experience, knowledge of strategy, and plain military education needed to meaningfully reorganize, redispose and position the armed forces for an active and effective defense of the country (Werth, 1964).

Shortly before the events of the Finnish war, Poland was once again divided between Germany and Russia. This drastically changed the Russian military geography: the western border of Russia had to be moved west. The fortification line running from Pskov in the north to Odessa in the south was now too far inland. Russia began to dismantle and abandon the fortifications, before a new line was even decided upon.

But other things were in a state of flux and disorganization also. And the Germans knew it. One example would probably illustrate the general state of defense unpreparedness at that time.

According to the then current doctrine, tanks were supporting weapons for infantry. Yet in many cases large tank units were physically separated from the infantry. Since they were intended to operate together, the infantry received spare parts, petrol and ammunition for the tanks. Such was the case in at least one division, according to a surviving veteran.

Marshal Tukhachevski, before his execution during the great military purges, prepared an interesting, meaningful and functional plan of military disposition. But there were only a few specialists who could execute the plan. Whatever was attempted toward the summer of 1941 was half finished, poorly done or not accomplished at all. The government was aware of the situation only in very general terms. What was not sufficiently clear to the Russians was the extent of German preparations in their eastern sphere. Stalin estimated that he needed at least one more year of intensive defense preparations to become secure from attack in the west and in turn be ready to challenge Hitler. What could be done to gain time? The Russian answer was to purchase it! The Russian government embarked on a period of really tragi-comic diplomatic activity, with Molotov visiting

Berlin, etc. One-way commercial "exchanges" took place on a large scale. Large quantities of strategic raw materials were shipped to Germany. (Curiously enough, some of these materials were purchased in the United States.)

The Russian foreign policy attitude of that time appears remarkably familiar and "modern." Everything was done to appease the Germans; any move, any statement or utterance which might irritate Germany was avoided in order not to provoke hostility. It suddenly became unfashionable to criticize fascism and national socialism. At the same time the official Russian utterances concerning their own defense preparedness amounted to self-intoxication with wishful slogans about the "glorious and powerful Red Army." Political doctrineering about the invincibility of the "fatherland of the world proletariat" continued to dominate official statements, although on a somewhat subdued scale.

Hitler, in the meantime, worked on secret preparations for a "lightning campaign" against Russia. Staff work, planning and preparation proceeded secretly but was by no means smooth. Delays and revisions were frequent (Blau, 1955). The thorough planning was replete with deadly faults and flaws, sometimes of incredible simplicity.

Why did Hitler need to attack Russia while still at war with England? It is a complex question. One reason lies in the nature of a dictatorship: Hitler, a man full of preconceptions of his and his race's superiority, with strong convictions about the inferior nature of all other nations (and especially the Russians), was clearly full of hatred for anything that got in his way.

In his very special frame of mind, Hitler could easily convince himself that Russia must be destroyed. Having established that goal, his next task would, to be logical, consist in carefully weighing all contributing factors against negative ones. But that was not the way he functioned. Because of his colossal, absolute power, it was his experience that his will always prevailed. For this reason he felt justified in ignoring or brushing aside arguments against his decisions. It seems that dictators see no difference between the concepts of will, desire and need on the one hand, and capability on the other.

So all the facts which did not support, illustrate or substantiate Hitler's decisions were readily brushed aside. For instance, Hitler received information about an excellent new training program for the Russian infantry. In his mind that was impossible, since only a superior German soldier could benefit from meaningful training. Reports about the detrimental effects of the great military purges of 1937-1938 were benevolently received. Admiral Doenitz's argument that Russia, having no significant naval power and depending upon Germany for large-scale ship construction, would not be likely to attack was also promptly dismissed (Werth, 1964). Hitler's favorite argument in favor of an immediate attack of Russia was that at a later time, when the Red Army had finished its reorganization and the war with England was in an active phase, the danger of a "stab in the back" would be real. How valid that was is now hard to judge.

Planning for the campaign against Russia proceeded under the code name "Barbarossa" and began with the famous Directive #21 on 18 December 1940. The planning proceeded in a most thorough, painstaking way through all the stages of staff work, intelligence estimates, evaluation of terrain and its traffic-bearing capability; and thorough estimates of the adversary's military strngth, disposition and strategic reaction to a major assault. The plan called for a surprise attack of the "Blitzkrieg" (war with lightning speed) type — engagement and annihilation of Russian forces in the western parts of the Ukraine and Bielorussia, culminating in the occupation of Moscow. The main strategic objective was the Russian capital, which was in certain aspects, it was assumed, the vital hub of all activity in the country. Fundamentally the campaign was firmly based on the following postulates:

1. After the main Russian forces are annihilated in the western part of the country the adversary will have neither the will nor the means to resist.

2. The conquest of Moscow will constitute a great political victory, with a shock effect; it will also provide control of the main transportation hub, thus crippling logistics and supply of the front.

3. All the main objectives must be reached before the onset of the winter, since engaging in a lengthy winter campaign is undesirable.

It is not entirely clear why it was postulated that the Russian army would have neither the will nor the means to resist after annihilation of a significant part of its forces. Clearly, the German leadership had the wrong conception of the Russian mobilization process, thus underestimating its reserve potential. Most bizarre appears the emphasis on Moscow as a strategic objective. The amazing part is that the German leadership knew that Moscow had been controlled by alien forces in the past — more than once. Occupation of Moscow would not be a deciding factor in checking Russian resistance. It is also not clear at all why the Germans did not prepare for winter warfare! Napoleon could not prepare — he needed the "colorful uniforms"; the Germans did not. So why? The Germans planned to finish the eastern campaign before the onset of cold weather, which may be considered prudent, to a degree. But there was no trace of recourse to any measure in case the hostilities continued into the winter. And that was, as is clearly visible now, the main weak point of "Barbarossa." It appears now that the strategic significance of the drive for Moscow, entanglement in the winter campaign of 1941-1942, consisted in the fact that their "invincible armor" cracked, as it was often said. To be sure, Germany was by no means defeated in the winter of 1941-1942, but it would never again produce a strategic move significant enough to neutralize the effect of the winter campaign into which it was drawn unprepared.

The Germans drove toward the Caucasus. They made a lunge toward Stalingrad with insufficient force to secure and hold their gains. How was it that with all that planning the backbone of the German war machine was, if not broken outright, then at least cracked in the snowy battlefields of central Russia? Delays in the onset of the actual invasion brought it to the very middle of the summer (22 June 1941). The two months of delay contributed greatly to the future disaster. True, the German command achieved complete surprise, with all its tactical advantages. The inexcusably unprepared Russian armed forces had no plans, directives or orders except the catch-all Voroshilov type slogans: "Not one step back!" and "Fight to the last round!" Meeting only disorganized resistance, sowing panic and disaster, the German panzer columns rapidly gained ground and pushed east (Blau, 1955).

Besides the gross unpreparedness of the Russians and their lack of a viable military doctrine ("We will advance and fight the invader on his own land" — Voroshilov), there was, at least for the first couple of months, another factor that contributed to the initial success of the German "blitz." Stalin's propaganda had been hammering into the population slogans such as: "Life is better my comrades, life is more cheerful." Yet at the same time the population was semi-starved and subjected to purges. The propaganda was clearly a lie. But Stalin's propaganda also said that Hitler was a bloody dictator coming to enslave the population of Russia. The reaction of a large part of the population in the western part of Russia was, at the beginning, predictable: "It is Stalin's propaganda; therefore it is another falsehood." The bitter truth about the arrogant, harsh conqueror came out very soon. For once Stalin's propaganda was right. But for many people it was too late. The harsh treatment of its own population by the Russian government, the purges, semi-starvation, draconic discipline and shameless propaganda were factors contributing to the general lack of resistance during the first months of hostilities. But the Germans' brutal treatment of the population, mass executions, deportation, and public execution of hostages (Werth, 1964) rapidly changed their attitude. After the hope that Hitler's armies would bring relief from Stalin's oppression, starvation and purges turned to disenchantment with the new oppressor, who didn't even speak the same language, a large part of the population slipped into sullen, passive resistance, began to support the Partisan government, and refused cooperation with the invaders.

Most dramatic was the effect of the Germans' treatment of prisoners of war. From the very beginning, during the first months of the war, millions of officers and men fell into German hands. Mass encirclement of divisions and whole armies resulted in only weak and uncoordinated break-out attempts, and added to the colossal mass of war prisoners the Germans had. The German advance had all the appearance of a "blitz," and the only "care" for war prisoners by the Germans consisted of guarding them behind barbed wire under the open sky. The official policy concerning the Russian people was as cruel and inhuman as it was inconsistent and illogical: prisoners of war were starved by the millions — a painful, slow death. But Jewish and "Jewish-looking" prisoners, together with military members of the communist party and political commissars, were shot immediately. The whole ideology behind the treatment of the Russian population was based on the national socialistic creed about superior Germanic people ("Herrenrasse") and inferior people, for example, the Slavic people ("Untermensch"). A whole ideologically "consistent" literature evolved in Germany at that time (an example would be Dwinger, 1943).

The initial apathy (Magidoff, 1953) and chaos on the crumbling front, and the inadequate fundamentals of strategy applied, resulted in a series of encirclements and the capture of more than 3 million prisoners of war in the first 4 months of the war (Dallin, 1957). Most of the Russian armed forces allocated to protect the western boundaries were destroyed in the initial months of the war, but the rapid advance of the Germans gradually slowed down. While in the first 38 days there was more than 450 miles of advance, the rest of the offensive toward Moscow did not resemble a "blitz" at all. The remaining 90 days they moved only 200 miles against a stiffening, more organized resistance (Blau, 1955). With a somewhat infantile irritation, the Germans noticed the ever-stiffening resistance by "those stubborn Russians, who do not know that they are defeated according to the rules of the game, and fight, instead of throwing their hands up," as an eyewitness said at the time. The Germans also felt the ever-lengthening, overstretched lines of communication.

What state was the Russian command in, and what were the reasons for the very serious set-backs during the summer of 1941? Some, we have already mentioned, were surprise, unpreparedness and faulty Voroshilov doctrine. Interesting is the role of the Supreme Commander of the Russian forces, I.V. Stalin. The man's ability to lead armies was greatly impaired by his "position in the world." Stalin was both the most powerful and the most absolute dictator the world ever knew. That led to deep isolation, and the inability to seek, obtain and use the talent, advice and help of subordinates. When he was decimating his best officers during the purges in 1937-1938, there was not and could not be a single person to advise him against it. When Budionniy and Voroshilov were proclaiming that the Red Army was the most formidable force in the world, he readily accepted that slogan, as if it had been the result of a careful and impartial evaluation. Finally, there still lingered the Marxist-Leninist idea of the world revolution, which resulted in a notion that the "proletariat" (workers), when in uniform, would not fight against their liberated Soviet brothers. (A permanent official slogan of the time was: "The USSR is the fatherland of all the suppressed workers of the world." But the workers did not know this.) Since Stalin was capable of hearing only what he wanted to hear, Voroshilov developed a purely offensive strategy, as unrealistic as it could be, without any contingency plans, and based on slogans acceptable to Stalin. That was his survival secret. So on 22 June 1941, Stalin was to a great degree isolated from reality, at least as far as defense was concerned. In his very first orders he demanded self-restraint, so as not to play into the hands of "provocateurs," hoping that the dramatic events were meaningless. But Count Schulenburg soon presented the declaration of war to Molotov in Moscow. The next order addressed to everybody was to resist whenever the enemy attacked, and that was done.

What the uncoordinated, planless resistance meant and resulted in is very well known. What followed was an event of great significance for the understanding of how the mind of an absolute dictator functions. Stalin withdrew from all activities, cut off all contact with his aides. Deeply depressed, he repeated: "All was in vain, all the great work of Lenin, all the great work of Lenin and mine, is being lost. All is lost." For this, we have the account of a formidably credible eyewitness (Khrushchev, 1954). Never again did Stalin regain firm contact with reality, and never were his commands fully realistic — for example, his terrible blunders during the battle for Kharkov in late spring, 1942 (Khrushchev, 1956). Persuaded by the Politburo, he organized his "command in vacuum," shifting regiments and divisions back and forth, using a large world globe as his main visual aid (Khrushchev, 1956).

Using the system of commissars which was reestablished on 16 July 1941, Stalin introduced a discipline in the ranks of his armed forces that was unheard of in its cruelty and meaninglessness. The U.S. Department of the Army Historical Studies registered mass executions of small units for unsuccessful attacks (Department of the Army, 1953). The Germans were always puzzled by the repeated suicide attacks on their strong positions. As they describe it, a wave of starving men would be cut down by automatic fire, every man killed or dying in the snow. Then another mass would advance, arm themselves with the weapons of their fallen comrades*, and press forward. The astounded Germans observed that those beaten back and retreating were executed by a chain of screening troops. Eyewitnesses from both sides confirmed this "practice" on several occasions.

These wasteful practices were the result of "energetic" action in a crisis situation by a demoralized, panicky leadership. The Russian leadership decided that the harshest possible discipline might counteract the universal panic and state of crisis. So whenever the order to attack or hold a position came down, regardless of the circumstances, it either was obeyed or its recipients died. In practice the people were executed whenever they fled! Contributive also was knowledge of the treatment received from the Germans by prisoners of war. Besides the general state of panic, the deciding factor in this appalling waste of manpower was the general deficiency of qualified upper and middle echelon commanders. There were not enough capable men. The Stavka (Stalin's headquarters) gave orders, worked out on Stalin's globe, and the upper echelon worked out implementing details encompassing every trench and hill without receiving needed details from the battle lines.

---

* It appears that before the beginning of the winter counteroffensive many segments of the Russian defense front were in a critical situation. The shortage of troops and firearms was so great that men from the general population were pressed into service "from the streets" without arms or uniforms.

But signs began to appear that things were slowly improving. There was some coordination of movement evident, and gaps began to be closed by trained and equipped units. To the very end of the war, however, there was a gap evident between the issuance of Stalin's orders and their implementation (see, for example, Lomov, 1965).

Approximately half a year after the hostilities began, the Germans began to be seriously impressed by the type of training the Russian soldier had had. With the coming of the winter and snow on the ground that impression grew into strong respect, which was shared by most of the German commanders except Hitler. The German evaluation of Russian tactics, especially small unit operation, began to be very favorable. They were impressed by the Russian soldier's ability to camouflage, to quickly dig in, to march over long distances in winter, and to endure hardship. As mentioned, constant irritation was caused by the refusal of the Russian soldier to surrender. These peculiarities were invariably explained as characteristic of the "Slavic soul." Actually, the ability to march, camouflage, etc. was the result of superior training, and the die-hard attitude on the battlefield was partially the Germans' own doing (Department of the Army, 1950, 1953). In that connection it is probably valuable to remark that the German command was disturbed by a disproportionately high loss of officers during the fall and winter of 1941. The simple explanation, which never occurred to the Germans, was that the Russian soldiers were trained to aim their fire selectively rather than to rely on indiscriminate firepower.

The Germans could never realistically evaluate their adversaries. Toward the end of the summer offensive the Russian army lost a large number of small unit leaders; the officers available were, on the whole, mediocre, and had relatively little experience. But that improved rapidly. The Russian soldier was characteristically frugal, tough, unbelievably disciplined and obedient, and had had strict and meaningful training. His field equipment was usable and useful, protecting him in all seasons. If ski-trained, the soldier could easily cover long distances on skis which were functional in deep, light snow. (Neither downhill skis nor cross-country skis as we know them would be considered useful under the Russian conditions.) If a Russian unit used horses, they were the small, shaggy horses raised by the rural population since the times of the Mongols. They outlived and outperformed the heavy western European breeds. When supported by tanks, the Russian infantryman fought beside the T-34 — a tank with wide tracks and high clearance capable of operating in deep snow. The individual Russian soldier fought equally well in winter and summer.

Most of the German soldiers in Russia were battle-tested. Their officers had superior tactical knowledge, and for many of the higher officers this was their "second visit" to Russia. Their soldiers were well armed and well equipped for good weather and summer soldiering. Especially formidable were the excellently trained submachine pistol infiltrating units. But they functioned well only in good summer weather. Spoiled by victories in many battles and under the influence of Nazi propaganda, the German soldier was generally cruel and arrogant to the population. The German mountain infantry, the Gebirgsjaeger, although excellently trained, could not often use its skis in Russia; they were small downhill skis, impractical in deep snow.

With their original 3 million men the Germans managed to push to within sight of Moscow, where the offensive finally ground to a halt. Both sides suffered losses seemingly greater than they could tolerate. The Germans lost close to a million killed, wounded and missing, while the Russians had more than a million killed and wounded, and 3 million, according to German sources, taken as prisoners of war. Retreating, the Russians had given up unproductive, devastated territory, which was destroyed partially by conscious effort — burned and blasted — and partially by shelling and fighting in the streets. Most important, the Russian civilian population was mobilized to dismantle, pack and ship a large part of the productive industry into the hinterland. The Russians managed to dismantle whole factories and transport them by rail east beyond the Urals. This relocated industry began to deliver materiel as early as November 1941. Reserves and poorly equipped people's guard units were successful in stiffening resistance but not much more. The Russian defense was still showing little flexibility. Stalin's orders were bloody and needlessly wasteful. But the German offensive came to a stop.

The first six months of the German offensive were often considered by outside analysts to have been the most crucial for Russia. Many observers believed that Russia was almost defeated (Liddel-Hart, 1950). Many German specialists advising Hitler held his ear by reporting estimates of total exhaustion of manpower reserves, of huge materiel deficiencies, starvation and chaos behind the Russian front. The Chief of the German Army Economic Office, Lt. Gen. George Thomas, evaluated the Russian strength more realistically, but, characteristically, he did not last very long (Blau, 1955).

What was the situation, then, at the beginning of the winter campaign of 1941-1942? The Germans felt the increasing pressure of the refurbished, strengthened Russian units on all parts opposite their Army Group Center. Fresh units from the Far East arrived and were sent into action. Materiel and ammunition difficulties were by that time nonexistent. The Russians operated with short rear communication lines. All small units, brought to full strength with replacements, were operating with great tactical efficiency. Preparation and equipping for winter warfare were completed.

The Germans had overextended lines of communication. Their rail transport was impaired by the need to change the gauge to the narrower Western European standard. Their ground and rail transportation were constantly threatened and often interrupted by Partisan activity in the rear. The beginning of a frost injury epidemic was an indication of complete unpreparedness for winter warfare. (Frostbite can be completely prevented by simple measures and skill acquired through training. Russian soldiers were punished if they became frostbitten through carelessness.) All these factors compelled the higher officers to request withdrawal to positions nearer Germany. Hitler, exercising his power as Supreme Commander, considered a withdrawal option unacceptable since: a) giving up territory would be bad for the troops and for home front morale; b) remembering Napoleon, he considered it dangerous, thus proving that his analysis of Napoleon's retreat was faulty and historical information was wrong; c) most of all, he considered his prestige at stake. His famous orders — "Not a step back" — were never implemented. The central front was crumbling in many places, and instead of withdrawing to prepared positions many units were put to flight and to makeshift positions. That was more costly in terms of casualties and lost materiel than was deemed to be acceptable.

A curious effect was developing in respect to the relations between Hitler and his generals. From then on, until the very end, the gap between reality and his image of it widened. After giving an unfulfillable order, such as demanding that an understrength, underequipped unit attack a strong, superiorly manned position, he was often sincerely surprised when the unit was annihilated. Also, Hitler had a mystical conception of the German soldier and his fighting ability. The "superior race must be superior on the battlefield with superior leadership." And in his opinion, he and only he was providing the needed superior leadership. Hitler systematically dismissed reports about the superior winter warfare capability of the Russians, their tenacity, etc. Like Stalin, he accepted only what fitted his set of beliefs, and had, therefore, an inferior conception of winter battle (Clark, 1965). In December 1941 Hitler dismissed several general officers. Staff work, so important in winter warfare, suffered. The morale and fighting quality of the German army was in decline. The extent of the winter crisis would not have been so dramatic if proper measures had been applied. Advancing so far into the heartland of Russia and trying to hold onto the territory was a dangerous mistake. An orderly retreat would have corrected it in part. The order to stay and fight, if given to an army properly trained, prepared and equipped, would have been tolerable. But given the situation, the events of the winter of 1941-1942 were the beginning of the German demise.

All the work on Plan Barbarossa appears in retrospect to have been a mixture of wishful thinking, unfounded intentions, faulty information and an image of the potential adversary that was based on ideology rather than reality. Barbarossa was based on the need to destroy the enemy's forces in the western part of the country. That was good. But there was no alternative plan to use in case the adversary refused to allow itself, as already mentioned, to be destroyed west of the Dniepr River.

The plan called for the occupation of Moscow as an ultimate goal, after which event, it was believed for some reason, the Russians would not be able to produce meaningful resistance. Nobody apparently remembered that in 1812 really meaningful resistance <u>began</u> after the occupation of Moscow. Many German sources (Von Unruh, 1947; Philippi and Heim, 1962) mentioned the long, overstretched communication lines that caused almost insurmountable difficulties. The impression is that transportation difficulties were at least in part unexpected. Finally, evaluation of Russian manpower reserves, industrial potential and resources was significantly too low, mainly because Hitler was incapable of reconciling his image of Russia and the Russians with the actual situation. Practically, he committed the error of action based on insufficient knowledge.

As a result he was engaged in winter warfare with an adversary whose capabilities were superior to his. It is indisputable that the Russians learned their lessons from the Finnish winter war. Military skiing, camouflage discipline, survival and march endurance were at their best (Colliander, 1954). There were also numerous minor everyday difficulties a soldier never reads about in manuals but is compelled to overcome in winter. They constitute experience. An internal combustion engine does not start very well at −40°C (and °F). Its oil pan must be warmed up. Heating devices are supplied, but as a rule in insufficient numbers, and they also often fail to function. Many Russian soldiers knew how to mix gasoline with sand to create a controllable fire (on a shovel) to heat up an engine. (In case sand is not available, snow can be used.) The Germans did not know that. Many of their vehicles and tanks were lost due to failure to start. Many other little experiences, including treatment of animals, motorized vehicles, weapons and materiel at low temperature, the Germans simply lacked. And that constituted the difference. While the German lines of communication were stretched, overextended and frequently interrupted by Partisans, and supply of the front became haphazard, the shortened rear communication lines of the Russians began to function superbly. The Russian tanks, especially the T-34, could operate in deep snow with comparative ease. Another example of creative improvisation was the use of armored sleds, towed by tanks in deep snow on the battlefield. This made it very difficult to separate the tanks from their infantry escorts, and the technique was especially important in decreasing the fatigue of the fighting men (Corotneff, 1943).

To the unfamiliar, winter warfare is many unexpected bad things. There are new physical hazards of exposure, frost injury, dehydration and fatigue. Terrain use is difficult, and entirely new requirements for camouflage and evasion tactics exist. Precision weapons requiring lubrication stop functioning, and artillery needs new air temperature correction factors. Most important, motorized transportation systems perform poorly, to the point of traffic breakdown. Engines fail to start and over-snow traffic in many cases fails also.

By employing their winter warfare techniques, the excellently trained fresh Russian units became formidable foes. Their tactical advantages, if properly implemented, would perhaps have led to a total victory over the Germans during the winter of 1941-1942. But in fact, the Russian offense bogged down and came to a stop toward the end of February 1942. What happened? How could the badly shaken German army take the initiative away from the advancing Russians? It appears that the reason for this lag was certain organically built-in tactical disadvantages, as well as a nonexisting strategic plan. The political commissars attached to each unit (reintroduced in July 1941) supervised the commanders continuously and participated in making the few decisions the officers could still make without checking with their superiors. That was a devastating handicap, under which tactical skill was essentially neutralized. Strategy, as determined by Stalin himself, consisted in a standing, literally implemented order to attack the enemy — everywhere. The only course for a general was, after addition of a very few implementing orders, to order his regimental commanders to attack; they, after adding some more details, ordered the battalion commanders to attack, and so forth. This meant that the only chance for the individual soldier to survive was to fulfill exactly this command. One out of three things could actually happen after the order to attack reached the squad level. The soldiers could attack the objective and be successful; in this case, they would probably lose some of their comrades wounded and dead. If the enemy fire was very heavy the advancing small unit might be wiped out; in this case, another unit, if available, would be sent out to attack. There could also be the case when, during the attack, the survivors of the small unit would struggle back without achieving the objective; it was often the practice to summarily shoot such soldiers before the eyes of their comrades. This was the responsibility of the political commissars. The repeated frontal attacks, with their costly casualties, and the commissars' excesses puzzled the Germans (Department of the Army, 1953). They adapted very quickly to this type of tactics.

The large scale errors committed by the Russians during the winter war of 1941-1942 were mainly in the literal implementation of Stalin's orders. The Russian armies put on continuous pressure over the whole sector of the army group center (Field Marshal Guenther von Kluge). The evenly applied pressure over the whole front precluded the use of strategic reserves wherever weak spots developed. Numerous breakthroughs of the German defenses could not be widened and wedged open, either due to lack of sufficient forces or due to absence of initiative. While the Russians quickly learned from the Finnish winter war to broaden their cold weather tactics, and the Germans suffered great losses due to frost injuries, the Russian leadership had the serious weakness of lack of initiative and use of opportunity. Energetic concentration on one or two major weak spots would have resulted in a catastrophic collapse of the German resistance lines. Hitler's stiff attitude and inability to adopt a flexible manpower-conserving system was inviting a spearhead strategy. Apparently, the Russians had learned very little from the previous summer's mass encirclement battles. In the course of their winter defensive battles, the Germans left behind a deep, relatively narrow salient, which at times became completely encircled ("Festung Demiansk"). To the Germans' great surprise the Russians neither starved it out nor annihilated it.

In the German rear the Russians operated several very large Partisan or guerrilla units. Their size was their greatest weakness. The units established elaborate headquarters in the forest, had very little agility, were very conspicuous, and received most of their instructions from coordinating centers behind the front instead of from units operating directly opposite. Smaller mobile, independent units have a proven, much higher effectiveness in winter operations behind enemy lines, especially if coordinated across the front lines.

The errors committed on both sides are only partly reflected in the rather abundant literature examining the first large-scale winter war in 1941-1942. The official Russian history (see Institute of Marxism-Leninism, 1964) omits a good deal of the erroneous strategy and tactics. The Generals Rendulic (1947a, b) give an insight into many German shortcomings, while General Munzel (1949) gives an insight into the disadvantages of the German armed forces in Russia and the peculiarities of command relations at higher levels.

Eyewitnesses and historians of the whole Russian campaign often reveal the existence of an interesting tendency which should have disappeared long before the Germans became involved in a war with Russia. Every time a winter approached there were openly expressed intentions to occupy "winter positions," even "winter quarters" (?). A peculiar situation was created: pressured by Hitler to stand and fight and not to give up territory, the commanders were not in a position to "go to winter quarters" as in the remote past. They converted towns and villages into resistance centers with only sparsely manned lines in between. They created what were officially called "winter defensive positions." The strategic fallacy of such a concept needs no comment. In the years following the 1941-1942 winter this tendency presented excellent opportunities for the Russians. They no longer displayed the poor performance of the Finnish winter. There were often excellent small unit operations and good coordination, military skiing was good, and winter was used to full advantage at the unit level. The German troops, holding on desperately to their "winter quarters," had to be on guard and ready to defend whenever the Russians chose to attack. The "winter positions" were by no means relaxing and restful. To counter the Russian winter tactics the Germans had their Gebirgsjaeger. But they were not very numerous, and with their alpine training and equipment performed rather poorly under the conditions of the central front.

The Russians were able to outski the German mountain troops with their superb equipment and training. The large Russian skis, with low ground pressure (or rather snow pressure), were more adapted to military skiing. The Russian army had men and units capable of marching up to 120 km a day under favorable conditions while remaining combat-ready. Harassment became routine: deep penetrations into the rear, attacks from unexpected directions, etc., were frequent.

Other events of winter warfare interest center on the famous German drive to Stalingrad and the encirclement and annihilation of the German Sixth Army. Stalingrad was encircled and destroyed in winter. With snow and ice on the ground, the Germans were again at a disadvantage. Most significant, within Stalingrad itself, was the lack (relative to the Russians) of ability to take winter hardships. (Besides the Germans, there were large units of Italian and Rumanian troops involved in Stalingrad.) Also, many Russian units fought in white winter gear, superbly equipped for winter warfare. Due to circumstances well described in the literature the enclosed armies did not receive the promised supplies and ammunition. Also often described (but not explained) is the failure of the German forces to break out of Stalingrad when there was still a chance. Indeed, a tank column under General von Manstein was ordered to relieve Paulus, the German commander of Stalingrad. In a strained, very difficult march toward Stalingrad from the south von Manstein took off. The march, well executed otherwise, fell short of the objective. Only 32 kilometers separated Manstein from the edge of the Stalingrad cauldron when he was stopped. Short of supplies and gasoline, Manstein came to a halt, presumably to coordinate his actions with the surrounded Stalingrad defenders and await further orders (Werth, 1964).

The terrain in which the relief force marched was flat, bare, and sparsely populated. The poor condition of the road network was partially neutralized by the frozen state of the ground. The significance of a tank force march consists in the achievement itself (Lechens, 1959) but, as is well known, the objective was not reached. Why the objective was not reached will probably never be known with certainty. The official Russian Second World War history is not of much help (Institute of Marxism-Leninism, 1964); it simply mentions that Manstein ran out of supplies. This is true to a degree, but he could have been resupplied relatively easily. It is important to note that the Russians interdicting Manstein were limiting themselves to infantry action only. The Russians also outran their supplies. But they were fighting in snow. At that time Hitler was in a state of indecision. Paulus, the commander of the Germans in Stalingrad, never received an order to abandon the encircled city (Clark, 1965).

Perhaps there is not much need to dwell on the Battle of Stalingrad. Much has been written about it, but deep, detailed analysis often slips into lengthy descriptions of tragedy and cruel suffering, or heroism and self-sacrifice, as well as standard patriotic propaganda, depending upon the origin.

The facts, however, remain clear and straightforward. A large German force thrust east into Stalingrad. A large Russian force organized "resistance to the last man." Faulty intelligence and eagerness made the Germans overconfident — they neglected their flanks and were encircled. They were still poorly prepared for mobile winter operation and the Russians were the masters of the snow-covered landscape. Both sides outran their supply bases, but the Russians could function under the circumstances because they were better at winter warfare. The German High Command, probably Hitler himself, overemphasized the strategic and political propaganda value of Stalingrad, froze in indecision, and the Sixth Army was lost.

We might point out that a contributing factor in the defeat at Stalingrad was that the Germans were fighting a winter battle with false strategic objectives. The city dominated the River Volga — a major waterway important in supplying the northern part of the front with automotive fuel. Cut at Stalingrad, it would still have supplied the southern part. The north could have been supplied from the Urals and from Murmansk and Arkhangel. It appears that the main value of Stalingrad was in the name: to take and hold a historical city recently renamed for Stalin was for Hitler a prestige factor. And that constituted faulty strategic objectives.

Contributing to the Russian victory at Stalingrad was a correct strategic objective implemented by sound tactics. They noted a large German spearhead weakly secured at the flanks, and established the objective of destroying it. That was correct. They were capable of a large scale mobile winter operation and counted on it. They did not attack entrenched Germans in the city directly, which was correct. By tenaciously "clawing" at any tank in the field they managed to slow down and stop an armor thrust using infantry combat methods. Since all this was successful with a relatively low cost in men and material it was a correct operation.

THE SUBARCTIC

We have shown that the German plans for the campaign in the East had grave faults and omissions but a clear, openly revealed objective. The main objective centered on the central front in Russia and consisted in complete destruction of the Russian military force for the purpose of the use of the land and all its resources for Germany's own benefit. In that process, Russia, as a nation, would be eliminated, and the Russian government system would be replaced by German rule. A primary objective indeed.

The campaign in the north (everywhere north of Leningrad) had a secondary objective, subordinate to the main goal. For the present, its main interest consists in examples of perhaps not very intensive but still important cases of winter warfare.

By 22 June 1941, the date of the beginning of the war in Russia, Germany had a large force occupying Norway. Sweden was neutral, and Finland declared war on Russia shortly after the beginning of the German invasion. Together with mountain troops from Norway, the Finns began their military action. The German objectives were mainly to secure the strategic ore deposits in the Scandinavian Arctic, to gain access to the Russian strategic ore deposits in the Arctic on the Kola Peninsula, and to cut the north-south Murmansk railroad, thus denying the Russians any access to sea transport of strategic materials. The initial objective of the Finns was to regain the territory lost to the Russians in the winter war of 1939-1940 (Ziemke, 1959).

The theater of operations was difficult. In the north it was stony tundra, highly dissected, swampy and impassable even by track-laying vehicles in off-road operation; farther south, in Karelia, rocky, swampy forest lay everywhere. The area was sparsely populated, with only a few passable roads.

The climate can be described as cold subarctic, with a long winter, a prolonged dark period, and a stable snow cover. Winter temperatures may not be extremely low; the influence of the North Atlantic tempers the weather somewhat.

Transportation to and from the front could proceed with difficulty, and improvisations, such as use of reindeer, had to be employed. This and the insufficient force assigned to the task resulted in a considerable decrease in the intensity of the fighting before the onset of the first winter. The Germans complained about the rough terrain, and roads existing only on the maps. After penetrating only 10 to 15 miles the German offense came to a stop at the Rybachiy Peninsula (Degen, 1948).

The winter war in the Arctic and in the subarctic taiga forest was fought as position warfare. Most notable was the intermittent small unit action (Department of the Army, 1953). The Russians clearly conserved forces, consolidated positions, and carefully observed the enemy. They were weary of deep winter penetrations, which were always energetically eliminated. However, transportation difficulties and lack of sufficient strength prevented decisive action by the Germans also. It appears that the Finns, superbly adapted, with perfect knowledge of the terrain, were the most effective fighters (Erfurth, 1950), but units of the German mountain corps also performed relatively well. While winter temperatures did not affect the Germans as badly as in the central front, partially due to more sensible equipment, transportation difficulties and the abundance of natural barriers prevented any spectacular gains, as well as losses, of territory. It is very interesting that the ease with which the Russians brought up replacements was a complete surprise to the Germans. But the fact is that the "empty desert" had many forced labor camps where inmates were taken out as replacements on the front (Ziemke, 1959).

The outcome of that clearly secondary campaign was almost a stalemate. The main German objective — to obtain access to the Russian strategic ore deposits and to cut the flow of supply from Murmansk — was never reached. The Germans were too weak. The other objective — protection of their valuable Scandinavian ore deposits — was reached before the Germans even started their northern operations. It is doubtful that the Russians would have started a march into Finland to take the Scandinavian strategic ore deposits away from the Germans. The Russians were too busy elsewhere. The defense on the Karelian and Kola front sectors proceeded with a minimum effort, in part by local forces. The Germans exaggerated the need for the campaign and the Russians exaggerated their victory toward the end of it (Rumiantsev, 1963). Actually, at that front there was no "victory" on either side — either one could record intermittent success in a large number of small separate actions. The final German retreat, a strategic necessity, was precipitated and hastened by Finland's capitulation. Neither the Germans nor the Russians showed any clear use of the winter.

But the Finns amply demonstrated once again their excellent way of handling small units. Their military organization was such that commanders busied themselves with loose staff work, giving, as a principle, orders of a generalized nature. The main initiative was with the small unit commanders. Commanders of small units capable of operating for a long time without rest and resupply displayed knowledge, resourcefulness and initiative seldom found in the history of winter warefare. It was said that one Finnish forest fighter was as good as ten German regular infantry men. Descriptions of the northern theater of operations, as reflected in contemporary newspapers, differ to such a degree that one is hard pressed just to comprehend the fact that the area was a theater of intensive winter warfare. While one side reported patrol action and measures to keep the enemy under observation, the other side might report deep penetrations, encircling maneuvers and combat against fortified positions.

More fundamental literature, with the claim of being historical documentation, presents the same difficulties in interpretation, but of a more general type. While the Germans always stressed the amount of effort and the size of the operation, objectives and their achievement were subdued or not discussed at all.

An exact chronological treatment based mostly on a skillful interpretation of Axis documents, with an objective interpretation of the events, is given by Ziemke (1959). Compared, for example, with Rumiantsev (1963), who speaks about complete destruction of the enemy, Ziemke's interpretation, presenting a strategic retreat at the end of the war, seems to be historically correct.

This perhaps not so profound comparison of two historical interpretations of a winter warfare event needs to be qualified, otherwise the reader is due an apology. Can the study of serious historical works add to our knowledge of the ways and means by which winter warfare is conducted? The answer seems to be negative. What have these two authors given us in terms of a description of winter warfare skills, capabilities, its role, etc? Very little — most historical works are poor sources of winter warfare knowledge. Veterans' accounts, military memoires, and other personal recollections disclose the real picture of what contributes to successful winter warfare.

There is a need for enlightened command, which does not abuse the ubiquitous modern means of communication. Orders of only a general nature, advice and information must flow from the top down. The opposite, commanding small units from supreme headquarters, leads to defeat. (Vietnam?) Commanders of adjacent units may coordinate their action directly if they are truly "adjacent." Mobile action does not always require that. The other prerequisites for successful winter warfare are individual, covering every single soldier. We speak of skill, mobility, and willingness to suffer hardships. All this was amply demonstrated by the Finns.

Since the American reader knows the history of his country, and since this work is not an attempt to write history, such events as the Revolutionary War, the Civil War, and the Korean War are here omitted. That is American history, and writing about it may be connected with dangerous misinterpretations - let historians do it. Besides none of the sides involved in the these events displayed any of the skills of interest - those of winter warfare. If that is a misinterpretation of history I accept the blame.

PART II

THE ART OF WINTER WARFARE

DECIDING FACTORS IN WARFARE

The longer, larger, and costlier in terms of human life and suffering a war is, the more obscure are the reasons for its beginning and for its end. Official historical analyses have a tendency to present so many "facts," "factors," "relations," "influences," etc. that it is difficult to get an objective picture. On the other hand, it is simple to state that Germany evaluated Russia as a potential enemy capable of "stabbing her in the back" and decided to use the element of surprise and attack first to eliminate the potential danger. Was that correct? Yes. Did Germany act correctly? No. Germany committed serious errors, before and after 22 June 1941. Did Russia commit errors as well? Yes — before and after 22 June 1941. So comparing errors is futile.

It is probably simpler to look into what is often called the warfare potential ratio beteewn the two powers. From a military position both powers were dictatorships, with the enormous handicap of dictatorial minds operating separated from reality. Both systems had complete control over their resources. The inequalities were in space (Russia had more) and military power (Germany's was greater).

That quality might be superior to quantity was often postulated. Sometimes the quality of its fighting force saves a nation. Finland's superior warfare technique, especially the winter warfare skills it demonstrated in 1939-1940, preserved its independence. But that war was short, so the relations were clearly visible.

Comparing the Russians with the Germans we see the entanglement of many factors, and the overall picture becomes a complex one. We shall see whether all the factors were equally important, and we shall try to separate out the most important ones.

The terrain in the east is difficult. It ranges from steppe to northern swampy forest and tundra, and it is hard to imagine that there was any surprise for the Germans in that aspect. Since Napoleon's time the land had been very well described and, if anything, there had been some improvement since that time. The population density had increased, and roads and highways, no matter how poor, were built; the highway network became denser. Terrain difficulties could not have been entirely unforeseen.

The sullen hostility and lack of cooperation of the population was often complained about by the Germans, but could not, at least in the beginning stages, have been a serious factor. After all, no invader counts on the "cooperation" of an invaded population. Later, guerrilla activity became progressively more bothersome to the Germans (Hesse, 1969). It was very serious in the winter, when the large guerrilla groups felt their advantages multiplying. The hostility of the population increased to the point where the Germans could no longer overlook it (Clark, 1965).

Official Russian sources admit that the year 1941 was for them a period of great losses, suffering from inadequate supplies, retreats, and setbacks (Pospelov, 1965). We may say that from the beginning through the first year was for the Russians a series of panicky retreats, confusion and losses of men and materiel never encountered before.

It is probably very wrong simply to say that the Germans lost their campaign in the east because of "landscape difficulties" or the resistance of the population. Judging from their initial success, the Germans cannot simply blame Russian superiority on the battlefield. They were superior. And they said so themselves.

The political machine of a country, its supreme leadership, is the driving force which sends armies into the field and provides everything they need, including every round of ammunition. It also provides "patriotism," discipline, enthusiasm, fanaticism, and whatever else it can along those lines. No wonder, then, that a political party is analyzed for its leadership capability. From that viewpoint it appears important that many political analysts of unquestionable expertise see a considerable similarity between the two systems (Conquest, 1969; Avtorkhanov, 1973). Was either of the two superior? Hardly. Both were personal dictatorships supported by one-party systems. Both used terror and mass imprisonment to control the population. Both claimed the major role in leading their nations' war effort (Shapiro, 1954, gives an interesting analysis of the Russian party-army relationship).

And what about the two supreme leaders? It would be important to see whether one had any advantage over the other. We look for advantages in skill, analysis, perception of reality, etc. We shall try to compare them without going into a discourse about leadership in general. Common characteristics of both men, besides their absolute power, were that they were subject to open personality worship, were alien in their environment, and could not have been military specialists with cultivated knowledge. Finally, both used their seemingly different political thoughts for identical purposes. As a matter of fact, the two men studied and admired each other's methods. They differed in background and experience in power. Of less importance is that both had different manners in relation to the men around them. There is no indication, for example, that Stalin, an incredibly cruel personality, ever had the violent tantrums that Hitler did, as often mentioned by the higher German generals. But that may be irrelevant.

The absolute power of a perfected modern dictator contains terrible weaknesses, which may, under the proper circumstances, bring a system of that type into jeopardy. To eliminate the remote chance of opposition Stalin subjected his army to the famous purges of the late thirties (Conquest, 1964). His will triumphed. There was not the slightest chance that the army would be a threat to his undivided absolute power. But it also became a willingless, amorphous mass, able only to obey orders. Thus the catastrophic events of June-October 1941. Stalin, as is known, had a panic depression. Some say, recollecting Khrushchev (his "secret" speech at the 20th Party Congress), that at that time he had a complete breakdown. Whatever the exact events, after that time Stalin never had any real contact with reality. He commanded. According to Khrushchev he studied his dispositions on a teaching aid — a globe! But his commands were unquestionable orders and were often disastrous.

To Stalin, manpower, human life, was an infinitely available commodity. The same was true for materiel. In July 1941, Russia had to reintroduce the political commissars mentioned before. That destroyed the remainder of the initiative and capability of decision among the officers.

The lack of grasp of the situation, not to speak of analysis and planning, are illustrated by the disastrous waste of manpower on the Kertsh Peninsula or the attrition of manpower and materiel during the abortive attack on Kharkov in May 1942 (Werth, 1964; Clark, 1965; see also Magidoff, 1953). The "absolute orders" were costly in terms of space, life and supplies. It is evident that Stalin, having lost track of the difference between his will and the actual situation, could not accept the real events on the various battlefields. It took his generals a very long time to learn to modify the stern "Stavka" (Russian headquarters) orders into practical measures without losing their heads (literally). Stalin's "Stavka" learned slowly. But especially dramatic was the effect of experience gained by the Russian army on the battlefield. The great purges had eliminated the best leaders and organizers from the ranks of the Russian commands. The Finnish humiliation and the colossal losses in the initial period were doubtless the consequence of that. Cultivating the leadership of a country's army in peacetime takes a very long time. Battle experience develops leaders fast. A major victory for the field commanders, one which made them more effective, was the curtailment of the stifling power of the political commissars in October 1942. Cruel mass executions and court martials became less frequent. A certain pragmatism began to be detectable (Werth, 1964). "Prikaz" (orders) were now issued whose fulfillment was possible. The power of decision in details began to play an increasing role. An important factor, but one deliberately overlooked by the officials, was the increasing flow of lend-lease supplies in the fall of 1941, and especially in the spring of 1942.

Another interesting observation may be made in connection with the subject of dictators and dictatorships: the will of a perfect dictator is unopposed. It is expressed in decrees, orders and proclamations. The loss of realism apparently takes place with the impression of ease that arises whenever a report arrives saying that an order has been implemented. The habit of analyzing before ordering apparently deteriorates, the need to analyze becomes obscure, and deadly errors are made. This must have taken place with Hitler. Much was said about the character of Hitler — his "iron will" which, apparently, sent him into that multifront war, his self-proclaimed "intuition," and "strategic genius." Professor H.R. Trevor-Roper, in his Last Days of Hitler (London, 1962), presents a revealing picture of Adolf Hitler and finds many striking similarities to Stalin. (See also Gilbert, 1950.)

We may, then, make the observation that both leaders made costly errors for the same reason — their power was unlimited and the valuable critiques, analyses and debates could not be benefited from. The question of whose errors were worse appears to have been answered by the events of May 8th, 1945. But it is not necessarily that simple. The dates of major German defeats in the east reveal more. We must recollect the well-known fact that the major forward thrusts of the Germans always took place in the summer; conversely, the Germans locked themselves to the ground before Moscow and in Stalingrad in the winter. Could it be that all the strong and weak points, including personality distortion in both leaders, played a less significant role than the difference in winter warfare capabilities? That would be difficult to dispute.

The climate of most of Russia is such that a winter with snow takes place reliably every year (Koeppen, 1918). The population counts on it, anticipating and using the winter. Since times unknown, horse transportation of goods, products and people was considered better and easier if conducted on sleds over snow. Long journeys on sleds and long-distance sled convoys transporting commercial goods were part of the life and economy of Russia. Winter "hibernation," quiet winter rest in rural areas, is a figment of literary imagination. The winter has been, throughout history, a hard but productive time of the year. Winter hunting, for example, is a tradition, and it has always been part of the Russian peasant's life to load a sled with his produce and take off to the market, which was often more than a week's travel away. Winter warfare training for such a nation presents much less difficulty than for any other. We may briefly add to this that the greater part of the Russian territory where the Germans operated, or invaded, or intended to operate is subject to mud periods in the spring and autumn. Were these simple historical-geographical facts about Russia known? Definitely, yes — they were common knowledge. But the monumentally elaborate invasion plan "Barbarossa" did not consider this properly (Blau, 1955)! The poor mobility situation in the area in general was very well documented (Department of the Army, 1951). And the poor battlefield performance of tanks has been documented by experts (Guderian, 1952).

Thorough, intelligent people, the Germans undoubtedly had all the facts about Russia available to them. Why didn't they properly consider them? There is one reason that may be the answer: a man without the sense of smell cannot appreciate the fragrance of a flower or be repelled by the odor of decay. The Germans had no conception of winter warfare to begin with.

It is very difficult to make a thorough evaluation of all the events leading to Germany's defeat in the Second World War without a foray into the "exciting" situation where the use of sentences beginning with "If" dominates. (If the Germans had not made such-and-such errors their eastern campaign would have been successful. But then they would probably not have been Nazis, etc.) Also, it is interesting to note the entirely different interpretation of the same event, depending upon the author's political affiliation. Ziemke (1959) describes the northern operation of the Germans and Finns in the Second World War as a secondary campaign with a strategic, relatively painless retreat. Whereas the Russian Rumiantsev (1963), looking "from his own side of the fence," sees "destruction" (razgrom) of the enemy, and does not even indicate that the whole operation was a secondary one, strategically entirely dependent upon events elsewhere. Assman (1950), describing the battle of Moscow, sees logistics, weather, preparedness as the most serious factors leading to German defeat. Boltin (1957) pays tribute to the party and the leadership, and still regards the battle of Moscow as the most significant one.

In any event, no major military campaign was ever conducted without errors, and every error must be paid for in loss of territory, materiel or human life. If the two adversaries commit similar errors, then the error of neglecting winter warfare preparedness is paid for ultimately — by defeat. Indeed, both countries were dictatorial, both dictators had absolute power and a serious impairment of perception. Both had successful periods on the battlefield and claimed victories. The Germans were successful in the summer; but after the summer comes the winter. Winter victories were, apparently, what counted. It appears then that if all other factors canceled out, the skills of winter warfare were probably the most important ones.

MILITARY ART IN THE COLD

Within his environment a man functions, performs, survives, and thrives. Outside it, performance drops down, and survival becomes questionable. A native of the South American jungles survives perfectly there; brought to the United States he will have to learn to wear shoes and clothing, and any error he makes due to ignorance may have grave consequences. For example, improper use of socks and shoes around January in Vermont may result for a South American Indian in frostbite, amputation and possible loss of life. Properly instructed, supplied and trained, a native of any tropical country will function well, in some cases better than the local population.

To live and earn a living is one thing. To fight a war sets additional requirements. Briefly listed they may be summarized as follows:

1. All fighting men must be familiar with and properly prepared for low temperature, snow cover and prolonged darkness. This includes the proper use of clothing. It is surprising how much harm people can do to themselves by negligent and improper use of clothing. There is also a need to know how to prevent frost injury in cold weather, to have proper dietary habits, hygiene, etc. It is known, for example, that dehydration in winter is as dangerous as in a hot desert. Improperly trained people are tempted to use snow to quench their thirst in the field, which is

absolutely unacceptable. The skills of outdoor living (called survival) need to be learned by instruction and training. Untrained men in winter warfare are a liability. A commander may rely on having a number of men to fight, but they either die, or are injured, or become ill and must be taken care of.

2. A snow-covered theater of operations presents unique tactical opportunities. Skiers acquire an additional mobility and road vehicles must await snow removal before starting to move. Scouts and infiltrating troops become invisible. To take full advantage of these opportunities, winter warfare skills must be learned. A good beginning is to read the material found in the various manuals that involved armies have to offer. But learning should be accompanied by intensive training.

To the well-worn cliché that a power goes to war in order to impose its will upon a reluctant adversary, we may add that this must be done at the time that presents the best chance of success, at the least cost, and in the shortest period. It is said that a campaign must be conducted efficiently. We have already indicated that in temperate and cold climates the more prepared side will deliberately select the winter for the decisive battle. This may be done either by selecting the time to begin the armed conflict, or by avoiding the main battle until the advantageous time arrives. In the primitive battles of antiquity the weather and the time of year were not such important factors as they are now — the battlefield weather affected both sides in the same way. But the examples we have quoted also indicate the opposite: the power better prepared or adapted to winter warfare has the advantage.

It is important to emphasize that the winter warfare skills of an army cannot be evaluated separately from its moral qualities. Friedrich Engels emphasized that for a proper evaluation of the combat qualities of an army one must be informed not only about its materiel and firepower, but also about the degree of discipline, steadfastness and stamina. Most of all information is needed about an army's moral status to provide an estimation of the hardships that could be imposed without demoralization (1957 translation).

The need for winter warfare skills is concentrated mainly around the teamwork of small units. The main prerequisite for a successful winter operation is the development of survival skills. All members of a small unit must be able to live, move and rest in the open in any weather and any temperature. Clothing, food, water and shelter are as important as skill with weapons. The ability to march over snow-covered terrain, and to use camouflage and evasion tactics, is vital. Not all is achieved and not all is well with most armies preparing to fight and defend themselves in cold weather or cold climates. The clothing of native people in the north is light and warm; army clothing is heavy and impractical. Eskimos, Chiuckchy, Nenetz and others were able to travel light, fast, and over long distances. Before the change of their economic life they consistently preferred to travel in the winter. With the exception of a very few small ski units (such as the Danish Sirius patrol in Greenland) military winter mobility depends upon mechanized means, and motor vehicles depend upon highways.

To be sure, technology, firepower, and mobile and armored forces play a crucial role in modern war. Properly applied they help to win.

Improperly deployed they weigh a force down. But as we have shown, nothing is more disastrous than poorly trained men on a winter battlefield.

Briefly, the training of men for a winter campaign should include the use and care of clothing and equipment, the use of snow for shelter and protection, and the development of the ability to live in and move over snow-covered terrain. Customarily, in instructions, that which should be natural is lumped together under the term "survival" and presented as exotic emergency procedures, which obviously is insufficient for the demands of a modern winter campaign. Small units need to be able to march for long periods over snow-covered terrain. This requirement stems from the elementary need to be able to do the unexpected: people should be able to reach places where (and when) they are not expected. They must also have the capability of fighting at the end of such a march. A frequently made observation concerning skis is that specialization leads to uselessness. Skis designed for cross-country races are used by the public for cross-country pleasure trips, and downhill competition skis, or alpine skis as they are called, are a prestige symbol for amateurs. Neither type is good for military skiing. We may recall the helplessness of the German mountain troops in Russia.

The military skis in use now are by no means the ultimate design. Requirements for military skis, if written by specialists in supplying an army, could never be met. They would have to be inexpensive, durable, light, small, large. They should not sink deeply into the snow, should be good for cross-country and downhill, and should serve a secondary function as parts of a sled or shelter. The existing military skis of all armies are criticized by the proud amateur owners of alpine competition skis, racing skis, etc. (all are experts, with the degree of expertise determined by enthusiasm). Perhaps the skis used by Siberian hunters are what all armies need.

We may say for brevity that a similar situation prevails in relation to all other military cold weather equipment.

Camouflage, evasion and deception are different in snow terrain then elsewhere — any movement leaves clearly discernible tracks which last until the next large snowstorm. Those tracks can reveal, but can also be used for deception. All the old deception techniques practiced duing the Second World War must be included in training programs. Trail and encampment discipline must be learned and mastered. The Finns had a saying: "The lesson of bivouac security is written in the snow - read it."

The task of the tactician in intermediate and large unit operations in winter becomes less complex, but requires a large overall effort. All movements are slower, and the off-road mobility of fighting vehicles is reduced or brought to a complete halt, depending upon the depth of the snow cover. A large effort must be expended to keep roads open, and special equipment must be amply available. Very low temperatures adversely affect weapons and motorized equipment, and one must count on an increased incidence of equipment breakdowns and failures.

No matter how well the commander may be equipped with heavy vehicles and materiel, his success or failure in combat depends upon the tactical preparedness of the small unit. The untrained soldier is a liability; he may become a casualty before he hears the first shot. Well-trained troops properly equipped, capable of operating independently, and pursuing limited objectives have a superb chance of success. The tactical skills of small units in snow-covered terrain should encompass movement, offense, delay and defense (Deghtiarev, 1961).

In a march that precedes an attack, especially a cross-country ski unit march, objectives as to distance are set rather modestly. It has been recommended that such marches not exceed 35 km in 8 hours under average conditions, and 50 km in 8 hours under exceptionally good conditions (Gavrichkov, 1929). Those limitations are set to preserve the combat capability of the individual soldier. Besides swift ski marches, concealed bivouacs, and winter shelters in unexpected places, winter tactics require thorough reconnaissance, transportation of heavy infantry weapons such as mortars and machine guns on sleds, and coordination of ski attacks with armor (Sabaliauskas, 1971). The cross-country winter mobility of tanks was frequently used by the Russian army in the Second World War either by letting the infantry ride the tanks or by having the tanks tow groups of men onto the battlefield on skis. This way considerable speed was achieved without a gap developing between the tank and the accompanying infantry. Another interesting improvisation consisted of towing "armored" sleds made of logs to transport infantry. Swift night attacks by properly trained men were very successful (Vassilieff, 1955).

The attack of a small, mobile, independent unit must be swift and precise. To insure success, reconnaissance must be as complete as possible. Most importantly, the commander of the small unit should not hesitate to engage a superior force, provided that the attack is swift, unexpected and under the cover of night or a snowstorm. Ideally, enemy positions should be engaged by several small groups, in a coordinated but not simultaneous attack (Ljungner, 1955). It is important to conserve forces and not to continue the pressure if there is danger of being annihilated. Experience in the Second World War showed that if small units are ordered to reach a defended terrain objective, rather than to conduct a brief attack with the objective of inflicting casualties, the engagement often becomes too costly. Observations confirming these ideas are presented by von Senger (1954).

Since resupply of forward positions is difficult in the wintertime, it is especially important to have men trained in firing discipline. Fire for "morale effect" is highly objectionable. Each man must pull the trigger of his weapon only when he has a target. Resupply with ammunition presents far greater difficulties in winter than at other times. Also, the plans for each attack should include provisions for swift disengagement. The art of disengagement does not involve "a return to the initial position," which is most likely known to the adversary. A small unit with a permanent base is in grave danger of annihilation (Matsulenko, 1968).

While aggressiveness, skill, leadership, courage and the luck of the leader determine the success of an individual small unit, the task of higher command is significantly complicated in offensive winter combat. Preparation of plans, coordination, supply and support are more complicated in winter, and all have specifics to be considered. While it is true that a well-trained small unit may operate for a week without resupply (Fainshmidt, 1967), the rear echelon roads must be kept free of snow and frequently reopened; many vital supply items must be protected from frost. One must consider that in winter there are more frequent equipment breakdowns. For this reason, special skill and experience are required from higher command (Zakharov, 1967). Winter combat brings out the need for warm shelter in man and machine. Certain small repairs normally done "at the roadside" in warm weather become an almost impossible task in winter.

There is also the tragic fate of the wounded soldier on the winter battlefield. The importance of keeping him warm is obvious, but the opportunity to do so is limited. Exposure and frost injury is an ever-present danger. The Russian experience indicates that prevention and training minimize it.

Offensive infantry combat, with tank support, is very effective if deliberate field fortifications must be penetrated. By the nature of things, however, the approach of the tanks, their very presence, often eliminates the surprise element and new factors must be considered. As mentioned, an operational limit is imposed upon overland movement of tanks, depending upon the depth and density of the snow cover as well as the slope of the terrain. Shamshurov (1969) observed that in flat terrain medium tanks can negotiate slopes of 15° with a maximum snow cover of 35 cm at a density of 0.25 g/cm^3. Russian heavy tanks are capable of operating in 80 cm of snow at 0.20 g/cm^3 and in up to 90 cm of 0.25-g/cm^3 snow in flat terrain. On a 15° slope, 45 cm of snow stops a heavy tank. This restricts offensive tank operation and limits it mainly to ridges and elevated terain with less snow on the ground. German tacticians consider tank forces sufficiently flexible under winter conditions, provided that rear echelon roads are open, support is available, and personnel at all levels are well enough trained (Lechens, 1959). It appears that the most important element contributing to success on the battlefield in the winter is mobility (Grouzdev, 1944).

An attack with a small unit supported by tanks requires careful coordination of movement and fire. Both infantry and armor must engage the adversary simultaneously, yet to move with the troops may expose the machines to a higher risk from the adversary's anti-tank fire. Depending upon the circumstances, with travel speed being the dominant factor, the infantry must have a head start. The commander's skill consists in selecting terrain cover for the tanks that affords the possibility of support fire (Lechens, 1959). The Russian army is very attentive to winter training (Limno, 1973), and it is considered most important to develop coordination between small infantry units and armor. Also, northern armies carefully collect data on the constantly changing properties of minefields and obstacles. After a minefield is laid, a snowfall of 20-30 cm makes it passable to skiers and very often to tanks also. Plunger type mines frequently fail when their mechanisms become immobilized by ice accumulation. An adversary on the defensive may be expected to construct protective structures and position fortifications of a more or less deliberate nature (the borderline between deliberate and hasty fortifications is elusive). Attacking and attempting to reduce permanent or deliberate fortifications in winter may have tactical disadvantages. The leadership must explore the possibilities of mobility to see whether there is an advantage in swiftly bypassing the stationary adversary and cutting his lifelines (Erfurth, 1951).

A new element in winter warfare tactics is the defense of reverse slope positions. This presents less opportunity for controlled fire by the attacking side and a chance to separate armor from foot soldiers (see Biblioteka Ofitsera, 1966). An advantage for the attacking skiers may be

the increased speed of approach. Most important for a small unit is the
selection of a position which permits fast disengagement — to hold a
position "at any cost," or to become pinned down and annihilated, is under
all circumstances inefficient and must be avoided. Ideal defensive combat
is a series of swift attacks and withdrawals. There is great tactical
advantage in a series of lateral withdrawals and renewed attacks, all
conducted in rapid succession. In this way small units may slow down or
completely stop superior forces, which may then become targets for aircraft
or heavy weapons (Zhukov, 1971; Sorokin, 1939). While mobility in flexible
defense is an assurance of survival for small units, marching, resting and
occupying defensive positions require greater camouflage skills and discipline in winter than during warm seasons (Anonymous, 1941; Sander, 1959).
Enemy scouts, and especially airborne reconnaissance, easily detect tracks
in the snow. Laying false tracks; setting up false (decoy) positions,
campfires and smoke; and white camouflage have all been used successfully
to thwart an observing adversary (Zhukov, 1971). Since winter detection
became not only an art but a science (Gurevich and Pucheiko, 1945),
evasion, camouflage and decoy techniques have required more training than
before.

Defensive tactics at the division level are in no way like the mobile
warfare of a small unit. The modern concept of defense in depth visualizes
a line up to 46 km long for a division deployed along such a natural
barrier as a major river (Lysukhin, 1968). Prepared positions, obstacles
and minefields extend 16 km in front of the main line. A division in a
defensive position prepares a sufficient number of alternate fortified
positions to allow for flexibility and independent action by small units

within the overall mission. In most cases the role of a river as a natural obstacle does not decrease significantly in the winter. To attack a defending division heavy weapons and armor are needed, and that requires thick ice, which usually takes a prolonged cold period to form. Also, an ice cover can easily be weakened, destroyed and filled with obstacles. If the river position dominates the approaches the adversary has to use, the defense becomes less flexible than in the case where the defender has to operate on a flat shore with few natural barriers. In the latter case an active, flexible defense with maximum operational freedom for small units becomes advantageous.

The principle of active, flexible defense does not preclude deliberate or hasty terrain fortification and improvement. Foreign experts stress the importance of terrain preparation — construction of artificial obstacles and protective positions (Shamshurov, 1969). There are many methods of wintertime obstacle construction that are both quick and effective. An uphill road can be made impassable for tanks and vehicles simply by piling snow on it; a hill cannot be climbed if it has been iced; a frozen log barricade must be skillfully blasted away. In principle, preparation of deliberate fortified positions is not much different in winter than at other times of the year, except that in winter the frozen ground must be blasted by explosives and more heavy equipment must be used per unit of volume removed. There is also the problem of visibility: against the white snow background excavation activity, especially blasting, is visible at great distances, both from the air and from the ground. "Digging-in" by an individual soldier is almost impossible in frozen ground. Many armies have developed "magic" individual foxhole-blasting explosive charges, but no matter how confident their descriptions sound, or how many rewards have been earned by their developers, explosive excavation of foxholes is impractical. When or if the real need for them arives, and they are used, they may kill as many soldiers as they protect. Digging into frozen ground is a formidable task. But if proper training and tactics are provided there may be no need for it in combat on snow-covered terrain! Mobile ski operations — swift attack and withdrawal — do not require excavations, and preclude permanent defensive positions. A zone of entrenchments, emplacements and foxholes deliberately blasted, dug or "excavated" in frozen ground and occupied by immobilized soldiers waiting to answer enemy fire is ineffective, to say the least.

In contrast, the men could be on skis, moving swiftly to upset and disturb the approaching enemy with more effect. Infantry, including motorized infantry equipped with vehicles capable of over-snow movement, does not find winter to be an especially formidable obstacle (Frashe, 1976). Russian military doctrine points out readily that winter brings more requirements of a logistical nature, slows down all larger scale movements, and increases the need for supplies. For this reason training and equipment are designed so that winter will be less of a handicap than it will be for a potential adversary.

The subject of training deserves one more consideration: a soldier trained in winter is also a good summer fighter; trained only in summer he is helpless in winter.

SOME MILITARY PROPERTIES OF SNOW

Except on high mountains, glaciers, and permanent ice caps, snow cover on the ground is a seasonal phenomenon. Most snow cover develops in the Northern Hemisphere. In the Southern Hemisphere, except on the Antarctic continent, winter snow is restricted to high elevations. About half the world has moderate or so-called cold climates where there is snow on the ground in winter. Most of the regions of potential large scale military conflict also have snow on the ground in the winter. Recurrence of snow cover ranges from episodic to sporadic to fully predictable, and depths from a few centimeters to 80 centimeters, depending upon the climate and latitude. In the high Arctic, with the dry climate of a desert, snow is most persistent, but hardly forms a cover; it is normally found in drifts behind obstacles. The global distribution and seasonal formation of snow cover have still been insufficiently studied (Richter, 1960).
A snow cover may be deep or shallow; it may last for a large part of the year or it may cover the surface only briefly, in all cases being an integral part of the climate (Koeppen, 1918).

Deposited snow may be dense and compact, or light and incohesive. Individual grains may be coarse or very fine. In military reconnaissance, observations on depth and the capacity to support over-snow vehicles and military skiers must be routinely collected. Researchers distinguish grain size, density, hardness, stratification, crusts, internal hoarfrost, and temperature of a layer of natural snow. After deposition a snow cover changes its density, hardness increases, contacts between grains become stronger. It is said the snow undergoes a metamorphosis. The density of a light snow increases under any mechanical influence and, since any mechanical process is accompanied by break-up of a large number of grains, reworked snow hardens appreciably. Densification by compaction and reworking has its theoretical limit — that of ice (0.9 g/cm^3). Reworked snow is firm, can be handled, and can be used to make a comfortable shelter. The snow house used by eskimos, the so-called igloo (the word means house), is always made from dense, hard snow, found in drifts. Various types of compacted, processed and reworked snow were studied by Bader and Kuroiwa (1962). The properties, limitations and uses of snow are given by Mellor (1964). Yosida (1958) and Kuz'min (1957) discuss snow cover on the ground.

Interesting from a military viewpoint is the ability of ordinary snow to attenuate the motion of fast-moving projectiles and fragments. To study this phenomenon a series of experiments in terminal ballistics have been performed. Snow targets of varying density and hardness were placed in a refrigerated target room, and projectiles and simulated fragments were fired into them. The controlled laboratory work revealed a sensitivity to density, but not to grain size, hardness or age. Hard, aged snow did indeed resist impact more than freshly reworked incohesive material, but the difference was measurable only at low terminal velocities, such as free fall from 1 or 2 meters. Temperatures, as long as they were definitely below the melting temperature of ice, say $-3°C$ and lower, also had no measurable influence.

Age and work-hardening were the two properties of snow determining the degree to which it could be used. Freshly fallen snow has very little cohesion and presents some handling difficulties in laboratory ballistic studies. At sufficiently high temperatures (-3° to -10°C) the cohesion increases in about a week to the point where the snow can be handled. Then target blocks can be cut out and brought to the laboratory for ballistic tests.

At low air temperatures and in the presence of a steep thermal gradient within the deposit, the coherence of snow does not increase. Moisture migrates within the layer and becomes redistributed. Internal hoarfrost forms. Such snow has the consistency of fresh sawdust. It flows from the shovel, does not support the skier or over-snow vehicle, and cannot be handled. Passed through a vibrating screen, shoveled once from one place to another, or disturbed in any other mechanical way, such snow becomes manageable within a short time and is said to be work-hardened. Another phenomenon of work-hardening is an increase in density. Johnson (1977) observed that simple shoveling increased the density of snow from 0.18 to 0.34 g/cm^3, and milling snow with a snow removing machine increased its density to 0.40 g/cm^3. Johnson also found that shoveling, milling and compacting snow to achieve higher densities becomes progressively unproductive.

Laboratory ballistic studies required homogeneous specimens with a large variety of densities. This was achieved by screening and mixing fine- and coarse-grained snow in various proportions, and placing it in molds of suitable dimensions. Handling individual target specimens presented no problems. A series of rifle projectiles and simulated fragments of various types were fired into snow targets.

Chronographic observation methods permitted a correlation of terminal kinetic energy with penetration distance into snow targets with different densities. It was found that projectile instability (tumbling) was important in decreasing penetration. Curiously, an elongated ogive-shaped small arms projectile seems to tumble only in one of two ways. In both types of tumbling rotation is around a short axis of the projectile. In one case the rotation axis is parallel to the trajectory of motion; in the other it is perpendicular to it. Any intermediate type of tumbling apparently decays very rapidly.

All types of bullets and simulated fragments, as well as true fragments accelerated by explosive ordnance, penetrated ordinary snow (of 0.3 to 0.5 g/cm^3 density) to distances of 30 to 120 cm (Swinzow, 1970a, 1972).

Another observation of military significance concerns explosive fragmentation ordnance used over snow-covered terrain. A series of trials revealed that it is very difficult to ensure the functioning of a point detonating fuze at the surface of a snow cover. Consequently, a round detonates within the snow, thus losing part of its fragmentation effect. The degradation effect of a snow cover may be significant (Swinzow, 1970b), even if it is as shallow as 18-20 cm. It follows that warfare requires significantly more ammunition when conducted on snow-covered terrain in winter than it does during summer.

Foreign military literature seems to be positive about winter warfare, snow, ice and frozen ground. All information is presented in an authoritative tone, as the "unquestionable truth." Military troop manuals and officers' handbooks seem to convey the message that snow must be trusted, used as shelter, and especially as a material to construct fortified positions. All discussions about snow fortifications are illustrated with practicable drawings and sketches, but depend upon general tactical instructions (for example Deghtiarev, 1961) for implementation. Hard to find is information about the degree of protection a given layer of snow will provide against projectiles and fragments. Yet paradoxically, Belokon' and Korneichuk (1964) state that a layer of 50 cm of snow (how dense?) cut ionizing radiation in half. There is also a sparsity of information about productivity. It is obvious that digging-in into unfrozen ground under the most favorable conditions is slower than doing it in snow. But, again: how good is it? And how much faster will the soldier get out of the way of a killing swarm of bullets or fragments? The problem is elementary, and simple trials can give clear, definitive answers. Military experts speak of deliberate and hasty fortifications. The question of how "elaborate" is "deliberate" and how "spontaneous" is "hasty" cannot be answered. The Maginot Line was a deliberate effort, and a soldier throwing himself on the ground and scooping out a small parapet is protecting himself hastily. Once again we must do without definitive statements. Nevertheless the need for straightforward, realistic information about the performance of men in the field and the ability of snow to attenuate small arms projectiles is acute. Without a set of meaningful, realistic trials, laboratory work discloses only curious phenomena.

David Schaefer (1973) took a group of soldiers into a snow-covered field near Fairbanks, Alaska, told them to shovel up snow berms of various forms, and carefully observed their performance and the results. He found that, provided there are proper tools available, one man can pile up 10 to 12 cubic meters of snow in one hour. The light, fluffy, cold snow, initially of 0.2 g/cm^3 density, became denser in the berm, close to 0.4 g/cm^3, and acquired a coherence sufficient to allow blocks similar to those used in igloo construction to be cut out. Schaefer found, incidentally, that the standard army entrenching tool, designed for light loam and sandy soil, is unproductive, and that the best tool for work in snow is the so-called "D" handle scoop.

Silhouette targets were placed behind the berms and automatic weapons were fired into them. The testing of the snow structures was severe: the weapons were aimed at one point, so that the projectile impacts were concentrated in a small area. Schaefer observed depth of penetration, erosion of the snow target, and travel of the projectile within the snow. Aiming at the edge of the snow structure resulted in some scattering of the snow, and sometimes in slumping, etc. Otherwise, the reworking caused by the multiple impacts produced densification and a notable increase in hardness. A snow revetment of approximately 0.4 g/cm^3 density was subjected to intensive concentrated automatic fire by a modern small caliber weapon. One thousand 5.56-mm rounds were fired into an area 25 x 25 cm. Most of the projectiles penetrated less than 1 meter and none penetrated deeper than 1.4 m. Schaefer (1974) also reports that individual rounds fired separately into a target not disturbed by previous impacts were found as a rule less than 1 meter deep and a light snow (0.32 g/cm^3) penetration of this type of ammunition was around 1.2 m.

What about heavier projectiles? They are also affected by snow. The effect is multifarious and can, as will be shown, be very serious. Explosive fragmentation rounds — hand grenades, rifle grenades, fragmentation mortars and artillery shells — if fired into snow-covered terrain never detonate at the snow surface, as has been mentioned, but either at the surface of the ground underneath the snow or, at best, within the snow cover. The so-called fragmentation effect circle is small compared with free surface bursts; it may shrink as much as 80% (Swinzow, 1970b). The fragments, in most cases small, irregular pieces of metal (or spheres, in controlled fragmentation ordnance), travel only a few meters in the snow. Fragments traveling at an angle upwards have a large target intercept angle. So unless the round falls directly on the target, the target survives.

The fuze action of explosive rounds aimed at, and hitting, artificial protecting structures such as ordinary snow berms causes the rounds to explode within them. The rounds that fly through them are usually duds. Generally, an area bombarded with flat-trajectory fused explosive ammunition becomes "dud infested."

Modern armor-penetrating ordnance based on shaped charge effects, such as artillery, recoilless gun rounds and probably the Warsaw Pact RPG-7 antitank grenade, performs very poorly if the armored vehicles, tanks or armored personnel carriers are protected by a layer of snow. It has been observed (Farrell and Swinzow, unpublished) that the fuzes are triggered by the snow. The metal jet forms before reaching the armor, disperses its energy in the snow, and becomes harmless. A tank in ambush or guarding an object of tactical importance may become immensely more secure if quickly covered with shoveled snow. One meter of such reworked snow would be enough to protect against shaped charge ammunition.

All this shows once again that at the level of small units and the individual soldier the snow-covered battlefield has great advantages for the trained and skillful and is "the white shroud of defeat" for the poorly equipped and ignorant.

ON THE DEGREE OF UNPREDICTABILITY

How does a war begin? In olden days it was an expectable and predictable event. Feudal lords exchanged demands, insults and threats. Then their armies marched on foot into their enemies' lands and layed siege to their castles to teach them a lesson. An unexpected attack was something just not done. For the purpose at hand there is no need to elaborate on how this concept changed and how unpredictability became an important strategic element. What is important is that the sudden onset of hostility is a valuable asset for the aggressor. How much of its value can be neutralized by intelligence and direct espionage is difficult to say. We observe that wars, major military conflicts, are becoming costlier, bigger, longer and bloodier with time. The sense of danger has become more acute, but at the same time ideological conflicts seem to grow larger without triggering armed military conflicts as their solutions. This is perhaps because political goals and ambitions, clearly formulated as they may be, are now thoroughly camouflaged by diplomacy.

In other words, the aggressor, having thoroughly documented his longer-range goals in a series of ideological documents, enters a stage where he tries to reach his objectives by diplomatic means: treaties, export-import agreements, etc. are signed willingly and in great number. At this stage the practical (diplomatic) measures seem to contradict the overall ideological goals, but they serve the ultimate intentions. As long as such a situation prevails armed aggression is not necessary.

The peaceful side works, at this stage, on improving its social - economic system, increasing foreign trade, giving direct help in the form of loans and physical volunteer work, etc., all in order to gain sympathy and markets, and to convince others to accept its ideology.

The thing the peaceful and aggressive systems have in common is that both wish to spread their systematic ideologies. While the peaceful aims at instructing the people by persuasion and leaving them a free choice, the aggressive works with or against the leadership. Once the leadership is under control, the population becomes an asset to the aggressive.

The outcome of such a contest between conflicting ideologies and powers may be regarded as unpredictable, which is considered clearly unacceptable by the aggressive side. That is why a new diplomacy emerges. Its characteristic consists of an entirely new meaning of previously unambiguous terms. For example: "disarmament" now means that there is the intention to seemingly slow down the accumulation of war materials and weapons, but at a rate which will ensure an advantage. "Treaty" means an agreement about anything; the intention is to violate it (openly or surreptitiously) at the most advantageous moment. Incidentally, the people are never fooled by diplomacy (unless they really wish to be), neither by treaties nor agreements.

Somewhat apart is the position of the pragmatic peaceful (often called non-aggressive). In order to maintain the state of peace, spheres of influence, positions, partnerships and ideological postulates may be given up. To be consistent the peaceful pragmatist must be prepared to continue his sacrifice until there is no longer need for an armed conflict. Peace at any price, however, is defeat. For this reason, the process of appeasement, as it is called, does have its limits. Unfortunately, those limits are very difficult to predict. The aggressive is not limited in his appetite for advantages, as long as he is achieving his goals one at a time, and the process appears to him more efficient than a military conflict would be. As long as such a situation prevails, a safe, peacful period may last. Unfortunately, diplomacy, called the art of ultimate deception, which produces an avalanche of notes, position papers, evaluations and other difficult-to-absorb documents, cannot present a reliable evaluation of an aggressor's intentions. A good example is the period just before the German attack on Russia. Russian diplomatic activity was so intense then that the event of 22 June 1941 was a total surprise for them. Diplomats are often deceived by their own utterances. That is, incidentally, why diplomats are so often trapped in a hostile country at the outbreak of war. But they are always exchanged.

Watching diplomats actually increases the uncertainties of peace. Another way to predict the onset of a war would be through a strategic evaluation that answers the questions: a) Is the aggressive side satisfied with the progress of its influence and are the set goals being achieved sufficiently fast to keep the leadership happy? b) Is the organically aggressive side convinced of its military strength? c) Does the aggressor think that a war is efficacious enough and will not tempt a second aggressive force?

Answers to all these questions provide the only reasonably certain estimation of whether or not an imminent danger of war exists. To what degree and how intelligence participates in this type of evaluation cannot be answered. To do that one needs to evaluate intelligence techniques, which is a separate subject. Also, for some reason intelligence reports and warnings have so often been disregarded in the past. In order to stay with the subject, we have to be systematic in treating the subject of aggression and its opposite. In actuality there is a vast amount of literature available, so another reason, to be brief, is clarity. It is sufficient to keep in mind that there are aggressive ideologies, systems and nations, and peaceful ones.

The wars fought in winter by the skillful are interesting, important and historically significant. Some nations have survived only because they knew how to fight in the cold; others have been victorious for this reason. In otherwords, winter warfare has at times been the difference between victorious survival and the annhilation of a system, people and culture.

To clearly see the role of winter warfare is not straightforward and simple: history may be plain wrong, attributing, for dramatic reasons, a leading role to the misery of cold. In other cases a leader's personality, skill, will, politics and summer campaigns have clouded the main issues. Nevertheless, all the preceding examples show how important winter warfare skills are and what a great advantage cold weather warfare capability constitutes. One important task therefore remains: the peaceful must evaluate the winter warfare potential of a prospective aggressor. If the aggressor believes not only that he has advantages of an ordinary nature, but also winter warfare superiority, the situation is clear: a deciding battle will be fought in the winter. That decreases the unpredictability somewhat.

FUNDAMENTAL SOURCES OF MODERN WISDOM (?)

It has been said that reading history is similar to listening to a deaf man: one may hear many answers but not those to the questions asked (Leo Tolstoy, War and Peace). Searching history for fundamental material on winter warfare strategy leads one into the situation so aptly referred to in the above metaphor. The learned works give a wealth of insight on strategic thought and its development through the ages, but none of the great military strategists directly addresses winter warfare. Yet the thought is there, indirectly traceable through the ages, beginning with Sun-Tzu (4th century BC). In the "Art of War" he advises that darkness and winter are friends of the tough and skillful. We might add Mao Tse-Tung, who will doubtless be recognized as the greatest of modern strategists.

It is of interest to note that with modernization, dimensional growth and simplification of international relations, the distinction between political and strategic work diminishes which, incidentally, makes our task more complicated. (See for example a review by Bukovsky, 1977, or a selection of special strategic Russian works presented by Col. Scott, 1977.)

The interlocking of political philosophy, strategy and tactics points mainly toward the conception of driving forces in revolution and war. That there is a split in the Marxist ideological camps is perhaps less important (Lenin-type Marxists emphasize the role of the proletariat as the moving force behind revolution, while the Chinese political thinkers emphasize the peasant class). The trend toward emphasis on the military class as a political force with enhanced significance in the Marxist dictatorial system constitutes a new event. In the 18th and 19th centuries it was sufficient to study the leader (general, king, marshal) to see what his actions, successes or errors were, and in particular what his contribution to winter warfare was. Currently we have to read, see and understand a whole new philosophy, in order to evaluate any tendency in military thought and winter warfare in particular. But our main emphasis should be on changes taking place in principal ideological aspects which lead to some practical discoveries.

Of all the practical changes in strategic thinking, most radical appears to be one introduced by Mao. We recollect how Henri Jomini (1779-1869) postulated the need to deprive the adversary of space, to take away territory in order to put him at a disadvantage. Or Carl von Clausewitz (1780-1831), who spoke of initiative and the imposition of one's own will upon the adversary. (Incidentally, both these strategists spent a part of their active life in Russia and had a strong influence upon Russian military thinking.) Then Friedrich Engels pointed out that new interests motivate military thinking and create new strategic approaches, which probably doesn't mean much. Mao Tse-Tung, a strategist with perhaps the longest personal military and political experience, suddenly brought all thinking onto a new plane. He saw a new dimension for guerrilla warfare. Along with Sun-Tzu, he saw guerrilla warfare as a strategic auxiliary to regular forces, whereas guerrilla warfare had always been regarded as of tactical benefit only. The main difference between him and his predecessors such as Jomini was recognition of the secondary role of space: "To gain territory is no cause for joy, to lose territory is no cause for sorrow." (Interesting are his views on various aspects of the role of armed men in politics. He believed that violence must be creatively used (!), that the most revolutionary class is the peasant class, that armies can and must give political support, etc.) However, Maoism as a political driving force may be difficult and premature to evaluate now. (So is Stalinism.) Of greater interest remain his strategic conceptions that emerged in the 1940's. But that leads us away from the main subject.

What about winter strategy? By its very nature winter differs so drastically from other seasons of military activity that a distinct strategy must exist to accommodate the whole new set of dimensions faced with the onset of the winter. The new requirements on the large scale, such as clothing, shelter and ammunition, are recognizable, if not always fulfillable. New efforts must be made to prevent the breakdown of machines and slowdown and congestion of traffic, and to remove snow from highways and airports. New conditions appear: shorter periods of daylight, different conditions of visibility, new ways of camouflage, and others. New advantages appear: enemy armor becomes slow or completely stops operating off the roads, trained skiers become highly mobile, and skillful soldiers dig quickly into the snow, building excellent protective structures (Karatun, 1940; Chekotillo, 1943). There are also psychological advantages and disadvantages: the weak and tired are easier to capture, but the stubborn are less likely to give up deliberately prepared positions, and are lost. The most dangerous phenomenon, already mentioned, is the increase in the number of people who ingenuously find reasons to participate in indoors activity at various headquarters, including "platoon command centers," leaving a decreasing number of unlucky ones to bear the onslaught of the adversary. In short, winter differs drastically from other seasons and must be accommodated by winter warfare strategy. But no specialized work on winter warfare strategy has ever been written. Battles have been fought following the same strategic principles, summer and winter! Having observed what was employed or discarded in winter we see that six clearly distinct principles remain applicable during the winter.

I

To hold and control a territory is strategic stability. To do so in the winter is immobility. Immobility in the winter is delayed defeat and the territory loses its strategic value.

The implementation of the aims and purposes of warfare leads, according to the new views, not to domination of territory, as was the view of Jomini, but to the incapacitation of the adversary's forces. In effect, a space (snow-covered space) could, and should, be given up to the enemy if it causes him to be put in a situation where he disperses his forces and suffers increased casualties. A friendly land supports its army, also, when overrun by the enemy, presumably through non-cooperation, sabotage and guerrilla warfare. For this reason the main purpose of an offensive becomes not territory but the incapacitation or weakening of the adversary's armed forces. (One of the great defeats suffered by Mao Tse-Tung was due to his unwillingness to give up territory in 1934.) Mobility in winter warfare is a problem that differs significantly from mobility in other seasons. We think here of snow removal, which requires petrol, machines, and most importantly manpower, which means that there will be far fewer men available for the most important (and to an increasing degree neglected) occupation of trigger-pulling. No matter how good a snow removal program is assured, road traffic in winter is slower. That such a condition affects both sides of the "front line" is small consolation. Mechanized off-road mobility is always, under all conditions, more limited in winter. It can be shown that cases where winter (mainly frost) opens new opportunities to traffic, such as in crossing swamps and water bodies on ice, are exceptional in all climates. The only mechanical means of cross-country transportation that benefits from snow cover is the sportsman's snowmobile. But that machine is unacceptable for military use. It is too narrowly specialized. The trained skier seems to gain the most from winter and deep snow.

II

Only after the problem of mobility is solved can the second most important principle of winter warfare materialize: initiative. Without it a force is at the mercy of the adversary. Initiative means many things. Forcing a superior enemy to deploy into battle formation before withdrawing is initiative. So is engaging where (and when) an attack is not contemplated, or denying the adversary a seemingly uncontestable position of advantage. On the other hand, time-consuming regrouping, resupplying, reenforcing, or redeploying in the face of an imminent threat disclose one's intentions to the adversary and are unacceptable, especially in the winter.

III

Offense in the winter is possible only if five- to six-fold superiority is assured. Superiority everywhere may be desirable but is not always achievable. The initially successful Russian winter offensive in 1941-1942 fell short of its potential because Jomini's second principle was so ineptly disregarded. The Russians failed to single out an objective narrow enough to concentrate reserves on and to drive for. Pushing back an enormously wide front dissipated their efforts and they were stopped. How to achieve, then, local superiority when a sensible objective is recognized? Events during the Second World War showed that the Russians finally learned that also. When a major breakthrough objective is recognized, chances are that the reserves concentrated opposite it may be detectable and become known to the adversary. Since holding a "front" to the left and right of the potential thrust direction requires less force than rolling it back, concentration for the needed effort may be achieved by skillful lateral motion. This way local superiority may materialize. However, lateral shifts of force require perhaps the greatest degree of skill and control capability. Planning and execution must have a very high degree of precision. Preparation should incorporate the need for more supplies and materiel. For one thing, all ammunition expenditures will increase at least five-fold as compared with summertime. Also, every military need becomes critical in wintertime. For example, if a soldier loses a glove in the winter, it must be immediately replaced to prevent the man from becoming a casualty.

IV

As already mentioned, defense, stiffened by "prepared positions," no matter how elaborate, is strategically a postponement of defeat. Flexibility, with gradual minimal territory loss, may be the only creative approach. A positive illustration here is the Russian-Finnish winter war. A negative example is the Russian strategy in the winter of 1941-1942. Orders to "hold at all costs," as well as their opposite, or to prepare "hard" positions, a reluctance to trade territory for enemy strength ("space for time" is a meaningless cliché in the case of winter defense) are in winter unacceptable tendencies. The principle of manpower, materiel and strength conservation is most important in winter and pays off more richly than at any other time.

V

It is also important to see flexibility as a factor in defense as well as offense. Rolling with the punches, allowing the enemy to bypass (into Stalingrad, for example), flanking attacks, capture and immediate use of the enemy's arms, ammunition and material, all are axiomatic conditions for success. Most of all, many military authorities stress the idea that offense as well as defense must be conducted so that the enemy pays more in anything — men, materiel, ammunition, even hours of marching.

VI

Finally, superiority and surprise: total superiority must be counteracted by multiple local superiorites to make winter warfare meaningful. Any surprise, especially initial surprise, is important. The effect of initial surprise may last for a long time, but all effort must be made to eliminate it. The dialectic approach in strategy regards surprise as superiority in a qualitative sense. If backed by quantitative relations it may be equal to permanent success. This type of thinking can be developed at great length, but would lead us away from the subject of winter warfare again. One example is sufficient. The Germans attacking the Russians in 1941 achieved strategic surprise and local superiority. But by giving up space, materiel and manpower, all incidentally involuntarily, the Russians led the Germans into winter warfare. This evolved into loss of initiative, rigidity, and waste of strength; the rest is known.

The criteria of winter warfare strategy — proper aim, initiative, offense from a position of superiority, flexible defense, and strategic surprise — may very well be readily acceptable by western strategists. Single elements of winter warfare strategy were applied in the past, whenever skill and capability were at hand.

Skill comes from tradition and training. People living traditionally in cold regions require less fundamental training and can be subjected to the rigors of winter warfare with less preparation. But meaningful training brings the performance of individuals from warm regions to an acceptable functional level.

It has been said, apparently with a certain degree of irony, that the degree of overall winter warfare preparedness a military power enjoys does not depend upon its geographical position or vulnerability, its spheres of interest, or its centers of attraction, but upon the location of its supreme headquarters. Evaluation of that statement must be left to the reader, but considering world geography, the best location for the Pentagon would be Fairbanks, Alaska. Discussions and conversations on the various degrees of winter warfare preparedness of one or another power never lead to unanimous decisions. It seems that patriotic people with analytical capabilities always think that their country can use much training in martial arts under boreal conditions. (This expression follows the modern trend toward complicating simple expressions.) Having learned the content of the literature quoted, the present author joins those who feel a deficiency in winter warfare preparedness, skill and capabilities.

It is often stated that in the scenario (another very good modern expression) of the modern battlefield, with air power, motorized equipment, armor, artillery and rocketry, and especially modern electronic and electro-optical target designation, the emphasis is shifting away from ground power.

This may be considered true, only to the extent of peacetime war preparation. Indeed, the increase in cost between a muzzle loader and a modern M-16 rifle is not as great as that between a stone-throwing catapult and a modern tank or fighter plane. The cost of sophistication is high. But all the aircraft, armored personnel carriers, tanks and rockets are ultimately directed against the adversary's ground forces, who can move on skis in the winter and become more elusive than ever. Without friendly ground forces the adversary would come and chase the crews away from all the guns. While the cost of warfare may shift away from the infantry, the importance of securing, holding positions and advancing is still the fundamental tactical goal of the foot soldier.

It is also important to keep in mind that the winter has a serious de-modernizing effect upon military operations. Mobility of fighting vehicles decreases or ceases, flying weather becomes infrequent, daylight is short, etc.

Much has been said about the technological saturation of the modern battlefield, and a large amount of exaggeration is discernible. Ground support by aviation, anti-armor guided missiles and rockets, rapid fire, and short wave communications are said to have changed the nature of modern battle. But in the winter, aircraft ground support becomes similar to solar heating: it cannot be delivered when it is needed most. Rockets and guided missiles function best when visibility is perfect. The only tangible effect of small arms rapid fire is the need for more ammunition carriers. Short wave radio communications can be jammed and intercepted and, most of all, provide the opportunity for widening command power, which is usually harmful. The need to march fast, shoot straight, camouflage and survive is crucially important in winter; modernization has only a "coordinate shift" effect. Whatever new, sophisticated and "revolutionary" is introduced, it functions poorly in the winter. The introduction of small caliber tactical atomic ammunition (what is an "atomic weapon"?), called "weapons of mass strike" (Kissinger, 1957), loses significance in offense. Incidentally, the tactical employment of atomic ammunition would have a much smaller influence than is generally thought (Shamshurov). Therefore the role of the infantry in battle becomes more important during the wintertime.

UNCONVENTIONAL OPERATIONS

The wars of this century have had examples of position warfare and maneuvers, as well as a large number of unconventional and guerrilla operations. It is evident that in the winter the principle of guerrilla operation is most productive and economic. The Finns in 1939-1940 had both extensive deliberate fortifications and excellently trained and motivated mobile forces operating with a high degree of efficiency. While the fortified positions were eventually defeated, and many men were sacrificed to hold them, the units practicing flexible mobile winter warfare inflicted huge losses on the attacking enemy and finally ceased fire only on orders from their high command.

Conventionally one thinks of guerrilla warfare as a military operation behind enemy lines. This may be true if a well-discernible front line is established and the military situation is, or is approaching, position warfare. However, under many circumstances discernible "front lines" may not even materialize. The previously mentioned mobile battle of Suomussalmi is an example of a successful unconventional mobile operation. Had the Finns had a larger number of men available, and had the Finnish soldiers been trained only in conventional warfare, they probably would have met the onslaught of the first Russian force by digging trenches and emplacements of all sorts and establishing fortified positions. It is certainly conceivable that the Russians would have been stopped after advancing a very short distance, would have had relatively smaller losses, and would have evaluated the situation, found a solution and eventually reached their objective. Instead, the Finns used unconventional warfare and were successful. In counting on a conventional reaction to their assault, the Russians made an error. It cost them two divisions!

We are using the two terms "conventional" and "unconventional" as direct opposites. That may not be entirely justifiable. If attacking in square formation, wearing uniforms and occupying trenches is conventional and any other type of warfare is unconventional the issue is clouded. But just observing the past we may see a few characteristics of the type of warfare called "unconventional," enough that we feel justified in removing the "conventional" label applied at first glance.

Normally, when a conflict between two powers or groups of powers must be solved by military means, neither knows what his chance of success is. Then they engage in "conventional" warfare. If the weaker or the weakened has not the will, means or strength to resist, he is defeated by conventional means. If the one that is weaker in the first place has no intention of being defeated, and therefore has the will to fight, he must engage in unconventional warfare. (This warfare is the best for wintertime!) In strategy, nothing is for free. Therefore, the weaker one, or the one in the weaker position, must be willing to give up territory, and often population. What is gained in return for that sacrifice? Reduction in enemy strength in terms of manpower and war supplies, and time.

Whether or not this warfare is conducted by regulars using flexible defensive or offensive tactics or by guerrillas "behind the lines" is not very relevant. It is important to note that a significant amount of skill, knowledge and experience has been accumulated in the strategy and tactics of irregular warfare. It is applicable where the soldiers and the population have the will to resist, are unwilling to consider themselves conquered, defeated or occupied, and have territory to give up.

In China, Viet-Nam, Russia and Finland experience in irregular warfare has been accumulated. Part of that knowledge is applicable in winter campaigns. Three principles are universally applicable in winter guerrilla warfare: 1) The enemy pays more. 2) Do not hold on to territory. 3) A guerrilla force is the auxiliary to a regular force. Being subordinate to regulars, guerrillas receive guidance and coordination from the leadership of the regular operations.

Seven tactical criteria of winter guerrilla warfare are recognizable from examples and guidelines: 1) Units must be kept small and independent but should coordinate their action with adjacent groups. 2) All action is kept within easy reach and must be swift. Occupation of a town after the enemy has been destroyed or flees must be minimal. No action must be undertaken without a realistic withdrawal plan. 3) Any action against the enemy must be unexpected. A forewarned enemy is not to be engaged. 4) Initiative must always be in the hand of the guerrilla. If enemy anti-guerrilla attack is possible, withdraw, disperse, cancel everything and reassemble in a sanctuary. 5) Logistic support effort must be minimal. A conscious effort must be made to rearm and resupply from the enemy. 6) A serious effort must be made to keep the population friendly. Population support through intelligence, supply, etc. is paramount. 7) Guerrilla operations cannot be conducted indefinitely without a sanctuary. Two types of sanctuaries are recognized — friendly territory, not controlled by the adversary, and temporary bases of operation within the territory controlled by the enemy.

As is frequently recognized, the Russian partisan movement during the Second World War violated many of the above principles and was not as effective as expected, considering their number. The orders they received from Moscow were too explicit and had the same character as those the rest of the army received. The Russian partisan units were large and controlled large regions, with several villages. Consequently, the majority of the men never participated in actions. Strategic coordination with the main forces was often very poor. However, due to the extent of the movement it played a significant role in obstructing German supply through sabotage and harassment. At one time the partisan movement tied down more than 100,000 German security troops. Besides the size of the units, their main faults were a greater-than-justified reliance on central headquarters and an inability to secure honest and total cooperation from the population (Department of the Army, 1951). The activity of the partisans behind the German lines was notably more energetic during winter than summer. Landings by clandestine aircraft were more frequent, and supplies, medication, radio equipment and, most important, military-political leaders and organizers arrived more frequently in the winter. Anti-guerrilla action by the Germans could not be conducted with sufficient vigor during the wintertime.

The idea that irregular warfare is guerrilla warfare and must be left to civilians who presumably rise, arm themselves and fight the invader "out of patriotic protest" is narrow, naive and wrong. Winter fighting troops must be trained to be capable of operating in an irregular manner behind enemy lines (if there are enemy lines). Civilians need to be persuaded, recruited, organized, trained and guided, a complicated task that is difficult to perform if peacetime preparations were not made. In irregular warfare small trained units of civilians can be used in addition to independently operating military groups. In general, the boundary line between regular and irregular winter warfare must not be kept distinct. Most important, small winter-warfare unit training must include the skills so aptly displayed by the Finns, for example, during the Second World War.

What about anti-guerrilla operations? Reversing the seven principles of irregular winter warfare operations would be a rather simplistic approach and would not constitute a doctrine.

As is evident from much experience, anti-guerrilla warfare may be passive, mainly safety and security measures, and active, devising methods of neutralizing irregular adversary operations.

Guarding and protecting key objectives such as bridges, airstrips and ammo dumps may be the classical passive approach, and so would be selecting open, safe routes and avoiding places suitable for ambushes. Patrolling, and the use of escort detachments and blocking positions, are all effective if sufficient manpower is available. All forces using passive measures must be stronger and more mobile than the expected hostile forces. One must consider the colossal advantage of the partisans, guerrillas or irregulars if passive measures are practiced. Lookout posts and sentries freezing in the snow never know when or from where the adversary will strike. The men in the bunkers and shelters are idle and subject to what is called "cabin fever." It is not surprising that so many strong points, outposts and security detachments are so often lost to an enemy who picks his own time to strike.

Active anti-guerrilla measures begin when a territory is occupied. A thorough mop-up is perhaps the very first measure to be undertaken. If, after a time, the area under control shows evidence that irregular armed groups are beginning to accumulate, sanctuaries and bases of operation must be recognized and destroyed or kept under control. Raids and penetrations must be conducted energetically and fast; at all times the initiative must be kept.

An important measure, perhaps political in nature, is to ensure the cooperation of the population. The Germans, after occupying a large part of European Russia, initially had a large part of the population on their side. But ineffective propaganda, which did not correspond to native population policy, as well as harsh treatment spoiled their chance of retaining the people's support. In this way they lost an effective source of information and the hostile population systematically cooperated with the other side. Imaginative, sincere propaganda, together with a sensible, informed population policy are perhaps the most effective anti-guerrilla measures.

Under some circumstances it may be advantageous to give up a territory controlled by guerrillas rather than to try to control it with half measures. Removal of the population is a costly and desperate measure. It can never be properly done; there are always people staying behind. Relocating villages means leaving the most stubborn people behind and being burdened with the considerable task of taking care of refugee camps.

Most of all, the rather simple "if... then" rule must always be applicable. If the adversary chooses irregular defense, irregular offense must be practiced in winter warfare.

CLOSING

The use of the terms "war," "peace," "strategy" and "tactics" by many of the sources examined indicates the absence of a clear conception suitable for a definition with fewer words than would fill a page or two. In diplomacy, which also uses "strategy" in its lexicon, there are strong words such as "agreement," "treaty," and "contract." Their power is proportional to the tear resistance of the paper on which such documents are written. History studies such documents and interprets the events of the past as influenced by their content. This study ignored them. Since observations, and anyone is free to call them insufficient, indicate that wars changed the otherwise predictable events, and since we followed only winter warfare events, this work is not a historical treatise.

The art of warfare has become complicated with developing technology. Examples are presented, from primitive methods to the more sophisticated uses of technology in winter warfare. Again, since warfare during warm seasons and places was ignored, this work is also not chronological. The growth of a plant from seed to seedling to maturity is a cycle with an end. The growth of winter-warfare skills also seems to be a cycle, with its end not yet in sight. Also, it was shown that this growth has been far from orderly and healthy. Many growing branches dried out, and growth, or more precisely winter warfare development, acceptance and recognition, had to start several times from the beginning. Yet we have had only seven and one-half centuries under scrutiny.

To fight a war a leader needs men, weapons, transportation, suitable supplies, and clothing. The first one having and adapting all this for winter warfare was Genghis Khan. He also recognized and used the advantages of winter warfare. What happened to these experiences? They were ignored and forgotten!

At the other end of the continent the Swedes adopted skis for winter warfare. The effect was similar to that of the Mongolian cavalry — speed and unpredictability. Subsequent developments brought about heavy baggage trains that provided "creature comforts" to ever-lower-ranking leaders, until winter movement became difficult. Then, later on, the ever-increasing weight of artillery pieces almost totally immobilized winter armies. Other Swedish ideas — to use sled-drawn light artillery and to take proper care of the men — were glowing examples of progress in winter warfare. It took less than 50 years to ignore and forget them.

What was going on? To use a modern expression, dynamic changes in leadership affected operations. Large numbers of people were sent to the battlefield. How were they handled? In large columns. How was their movement controlled? Visually. From a "commanding position." And what was needed to enhance this control? Colorful, distinct uniforms. But from a distance any color except white is black against a snow background, and the uniform did not protect against the weather. The situation did not provide the leaders with satisfactory feedback (using modern non-language). Hence winter quarters.

In essence we see a succession of cases where winter warfare was either deliberately disregarded to make planning easier, or to have better "control" of the battlefield, but it may also be that winter campaigns were avoided to avoid the unpleasant.

Somewhat apart is leadership. Indeed, leading, commanding a battle between two large masses of people, may have, after a certain critical size was reached, become a formidable task sometime around the beginning of the nineteenth century. The will of the commander (from the command post on the hill) could be conveyed only initially: "start the battle" (by raising a flag or dropping a handkerchief). But later, commands to modify attacks, to change the course, to engage reserves could be executed only with difficulty and often too late. An example is the battle between the Russians and Napoleon in 1812. Had it taken place in winter it would have been complete chaos. But Napoleon should not have concentrated so many people on one battlefield anyway. In 1877-1878 the Russians had smaller concentrations of people and used the telegraph extensively.

So instead of having small mobile units operating with initiative and efficiency we see that the leadership had a tendency to use the developing means of communication to impose its will in more minute details upon progressively smaller units. It is an irony — the more sophisticated the communications, the more explicit the orders that go to the smaller units, and the less imaginative the independent small unit action in winter battle.

Dynamic middle echelon leadership used means to "interpret" (adapt or circumvent) such commands from the top. The result was success and victory (Lomov, 1965). The seeming paradox — improved communication, loss of touch with reality — is labeled, without explanation, as leadership crisis, and we encountered it on several occasions. We came close to offering the explanation that whenever the leader concentrates more power than his power of reasoning can handle, he takes mental shortcuts and relies on past successes, and his orders ignore reality. Only in such a way can we explain the absence of any provision for winter warfare in the seemingly thorough, methodical and logical plan "Barbarossa." Hitler wanted to finish with Russia before the onset of winter, and did not take the time to reason along the lines starting with "What if...?"

While the crisis of uncontrolled leadership may be explainable, we cannot explain why planners and leaders of so many major campaigns so thoroughly disregarded the winter warfare experience and innovations of their predecessors.

This is why examples of successful wintertime campaigns have been presented here.

There is an interesting custom in the western world. Authors, upon completing a poem, fiction, or a philosophical or historical work dedicate it. The dedication is a crisp statement expressing in most cases gratitude, appreciation or admiration. When work, whatever it may be, is completed, the dedication goes on the frontispiece. The reasons for it are multifarious. One frequently sees the phrase: "To my beloved wife, without whose inspiration the work would have been impossible," meaning perhaps that she did not very often mobilize the author away from the desk to do the dishes (?). (We only mean to say that the persons mentioned in the dedication never receive full and specified credit.)

If it were appropriate to dedicate this work to somebody, it would be the type of military leader who disregarded past experiences in winter warfare, who had more power than his reasoning could handle, used modern communication to abuse his command power, and was incapable of planning and predicting. Together with future leaders, we wish those past leaders to rest in a place which, tradition says, is much warmer than a snow-covered battlefield. They deserve it. Indeed, if all were skillful in winter warfare, who would need this work? The leaders who disregarded winter warfare made this work possible. Perhaps also useful...

PART III

ILLUSTRATED

NOTE ON ILLUSTRATIONS

There is a tactical reason for separating this part from the preceding two. For one thing, while all three parts serve but one purpose, illustrating the first two might actually disrupt the orderly flow of thought and so introduce some ambiguity. Furthermore, those of the readers who are professionally active in military science, with the purpose of preserving peace (paraphrasing the famous Latin proverb at the front of the book), may find this part sufficient and suitable to cover the subject. What we are stating here is that he who seeks peace should also prepare for winter warfare.

This illustrated part cannot be regarded as a complete and comprehensive thesis on all aspects of winter warfare. Here, as well as in the preceding two parts, there are gaps and omissions. We had to omit the subject of adaptation and adaptability to an evironment. We observe that animals must stay in their adopted environment. Outside of it there are only zoos for them. But people can emigrate from one to another environment. There is training, technology and inherited experience. Soldiers trained in winter warfare are good everywhere. Untrained, they are losers. The subject of winter warfare training, adaptation, survival and combat is fascinating. We had to avoid it — it would take a textbook.

Another omission here is the discussion, in this case illustration, of three traditional historical personalities who are often mentioned in connection with campaigns dragged out into a cold season: Xenophon, Alexander the Great, and Hannibal. We mention the reason for this in the first part. Here we may only mention a sad fact of very physical significance: the soldiers of all three of these personalities did not wear pants! Winter warfare without pants? They had to be omitted.

The reason why Genghis Khan appears in Figure 1 is simple: he seems to be the first who used the winter for tactical advantage. The last figure represents the main research interest of the author: terminal ballistics in ordinary snow. Snow is a most fascinating material — it stops fragments and bullets, and powerfully degrades fragmentation ammunition. Is the wish to share this with the reader justified?

FIGURE 1. Genghis Khan (c. 1162-1227).

With only rudimentary knowledge of the concepts of statesmanship and the art of government, this famous leader of the Mongols managed to unify a people who had a common language but little national feeling. There were two factors affecting unification at the time: tribal leaders were working to unify the clans, but clan leaders kept switching tribal allegiances. Genghis Khan unified and ruled the nation through warfare. A gifted warlord and leader, he was able to develop a new strategy and tactics based on masses of horse-mounted warriors. His strengths were leadership, the logistics of mass movement, and battle coordination. And although not the first to wage winter campaigns, he was the first to use wintertime to advantage. The purposeful movement of large forces over long distances, and the speed, endurance and stamina of the Mongols, introduced a new dimension into warfare.

Genghis Khan founded a dynasty of powerful rulers, and his conquests affected more territory and more people than any others before or since. Some say that the Mongols created Russia by forcing an end to the continuous strife between competing Slavic princes. In the lands they conquered the Mongols supported communication and trade, and enforced peace and stability. Historical works describing the "yoke" of the Mongolian rulers and the unbearable tribute they demanded ("Give us one-tenth of everything!") overlook the peace and order they brought to the land and their benevolence toward the church, which resulted in the growth and prosperity of orthodox monasteries. But the skill of history writing was in the hands of those who ruled before the Mongols. This, as well as their strange race, language and religion, was why the national memory of Russia could never interpret the period objectively.

It is said that their harshness brought about the Mongols' downfall, but in reality as long as tribute was flowing (Compare it with contemporary taxation!) their interference with government affairs was minimal. Their concept of government was minimal also, which may have been the true reason for their downfall.

FIGURE 2. The Spread of the Mongols.

In Mongolia, the River Kerulen (Hereleng) and Lake Dalainor are, tradition says, the sources of Genghis Khan's unified Mongolian nation. The Mongols were nomadic cattle herders and raised an ancient breed of excellent horses. Contrary to some popular conceptions, nomadic life was a series of regular movements made to achieve proper utilization of the two great resources of open land: water and pasture. The skill of the nomad was applied in the field campaigns of the Mongols. The preference for winter movement, the art of coordinating the action of large masses of horsemen, frugality, and speed were the basic factors contributing to the Mongols' conquests.

After establishing control (mainly by devastation) over China, the Mongols moved west. They ignored the Siberian forests to the north and the deserts to the south. Using the sometimes narrow grassland belt north of Lake Balkhash, the Aral and Caspian Seas, the Sea of Azoff, and the Black Sea, the Mongols reached Hungary. Marching in winter, using frozen rivers to transport massive siege trains, they quickly destroyed resisting Russian towns.

The Mongols left a lasting imprint everywhere they went. There are still Mongolian-speaking enclaves in China. Several national republics of the USSR are populated by descendants of the Mongols. Many Russian words and place names are of Mongolian origin. Historically the words "Mongol" and "Tartar" indicated the same people. Currently, Mongolia, Buriat-Mongolia, and the autonomous Tartar Republic are populated by people of common origin.

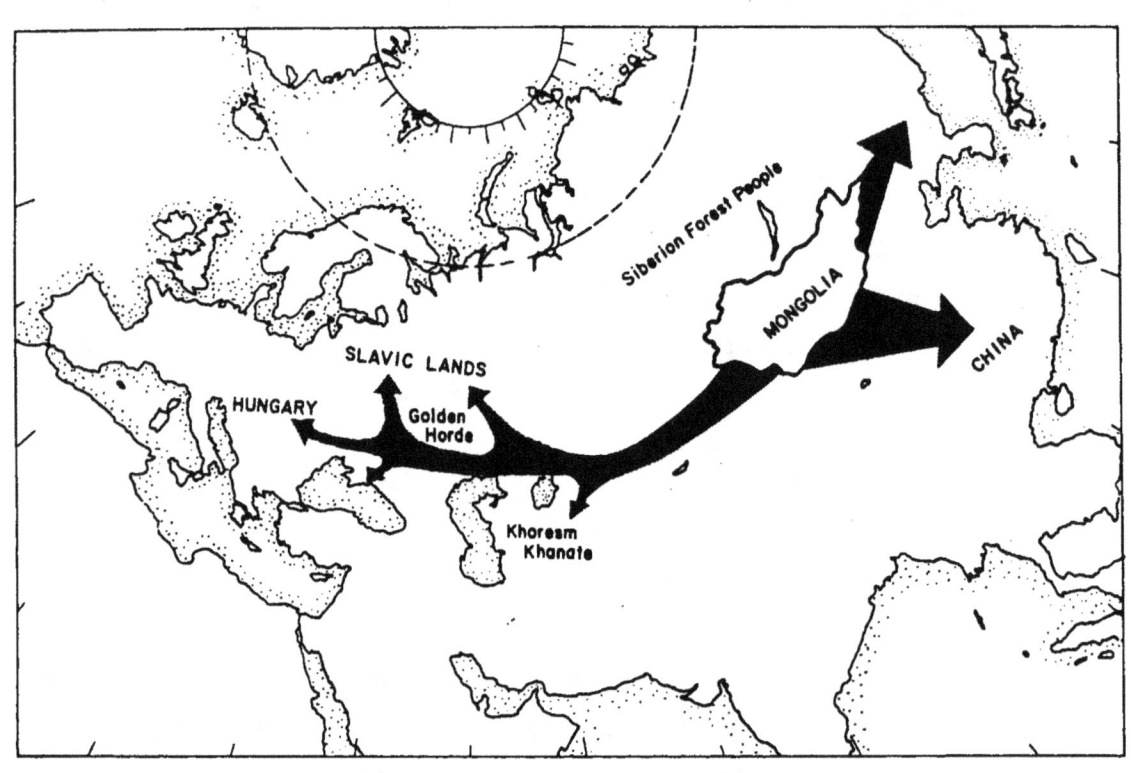

FIGURE 3. Warriors on Skis.

Olaus Magnus (mid-17th century) is the author of several books on various interesting subjects. Among his titles we find: "A compendious History of the Goths, Svvedes and vandals and other Northern Nations." While writing on wars in the north he published this fantastic illustration of men shooting triple arrows riding deer with arboreal growths on their heads or using large shoe-like devices on their feet, which may have been the result of a poor description of skis. (The Germans called skis "Schnee Schuhe" for a long time.) The part of the book that the original illustration comes from is entitled: "Olaus Magnus, the Goth, Arch Bishop of Upsal: of Wars Upon the Ice." It seems that the book's illustrator, relying on descriptions and narrative, introduced some distortion. There can be frustrating difficulties in basing graphic illustrations on narrative material. (The original illustration is cluttered and difficult to discern; this is an extraction.)

Skiing is also encountered much earlier in history. The chronicles of King Haakon IV (1200-1263) of Norway mention skis and describe their advantages. Skis periodically appeared on the battlefield. Ski troops had the advantages of speed and endurance without the disadvantages of cavalry: only waxing — no hay, no oats.

In modern days skiing has become specialized: slalom, downhill, jumping, cross-country. This has had some effect on military operations. Mountain ski troops are unable to operate on moderately flat land. Russian ski troops are mainly cross-country endurance skiers.

FIGURE 4. A Cannon.

The desire to drop heavy projectiles on an advancing enemy has existed since time unknown, and the means to do so were devised long ago. <u>Ballistae</u> were slow, cumbersome machines, but were nevertheless respected and popular with many warriors. Defenders of fortresses placed them in towers to reach greater distances.

The discovery of black powder and its use as a propellant did not result in practical artillery right away. The old cannon were erratic and dangerous. But the smoke and noise alone had a strong effect (mainly on horses). Experience accumulated, resulting eventually in the science of ballistics, as well as in advances in metallurgy that made artillery practical. Cannon on the battlefield could inflict terrible losses upon the closed formations of an adversary, literally tearing them apart and converting them into panicky crowds. But cannon had to be fought with cannon. Thus the artillery duel was created. Heavier guns had the advantage of range and had more terminal effect, but their increased mass resulted in lower mobility. First came restriction to roads. Then the heavy guns could travel only on good roads and in good weather. This became another reason for taking to "winter quarters."

Today artillery functions according to the same principle as at the very beginning: a rapidly burning propellant accelerates the projectile down the barrel. But the projectile is no longer a ball (cannonball) of inert metal, it is a shell containing high explosive for more terminal effect, with a complex fuze mechanism incorporating a variety of functions. Rifling imparts spin stabilization, which makes an artillery piece one of the most precise machines in the world (if we can measure precision as the ratio of range over terminal error). It is also a machine with a short functional lifetime. A gun barrel wears out after a few thousand rounds are fired, and each round travels through the barrel for only a few thousandths of a second.

Curious is the seemingly cyclic or spiral development of technology connected with artillery. Henry Shrapnel's invention added to antipersonnel "efficiency" in 1784. Motorization increased mobility (mainly in the summer). The short time that a target was exposed to an aircraft gun (or that an aerial target was exposed to an antiaircraft gun) led to smaller calibers and automatic rapid fire at incredible rates of 800 rounds per minute and more. These weapons fired explosive artillery shells equipped with sophisticated miniature fuzes at approximately 1000-meter/second velocity!

It is difficult to say whether or not there will be any breakthroughs leading to the discovery of new principles of propelling and guiding projectiles, and delivering them to the target. Probably the subjects of research will only be improvement and refinement of existing artillery principles. Perhaps artillery will be made to function better in the winter.

FIGURE 5. Gustav I Vasa (1496-1560), King of Sweden.

   Gustav I created a strong monarchy using confiscated church lands as an economic base. He believed in the advantages of hereditary monarchy rather than elective rule. Under him the country evolved from a rural society into a significant military-political power. He had progressive ideas about warfare, which he had the opportunity to test and develop in numerous revolts and wars. He did not follow the routine of moving large columns of men and fortification gear on cumbersome maneuvers. His imaginative approach ensured advantages in military winter operations. Fast movement, quick decisions and flanking attacks were some of his strong points. And of course winter itself!

FIGURE 6. Gustavus II Adolphus of Sweden (1594-1632), the Thirty-Year-War King.

Gustavus II had many new and revolutionary ideas about winter warfare. During his time commanders assembled big armies to dominate the battlefield and to impress the adversary. Heavy guns, ponderous baggage trains, and separate tactics for cavalry, infantry and artillery contributed to inflexibility and inefficiency. Gustavus Adolphus believed in speed, maneuver, and simultaneous attack at several places. In his small, flexible units light artillery supported the infantry. He even experimented with a light leather gun, but it turned out to be dangerous.

On November 10, 1632, Gustavus engaged Wallenstein, who was in the process of occupying winter quarters. During the heavy day-long fighting (rare at that time) the king fell, but this battle of Luetzen gave the Swedes a victory nevertheless.

Under him Sweden was transformed into a great European power.

Konung GUSTAF II ADOLF

FIGURE 7. The Winter Battle of Tuttlingen.

Two contemporary maps illustrate the 1643 winter battle of Tuttlingen (or Tutlingen, or Dutlingen) on the Danube River (or Donau, or Donaw, or Thonaw). Such "Relations" or "Delineations" were often printed on large sheets and displayed in market places, where people gathered and listened to a "Presentierer" with a pointer explain the event. Comparison of the two documents reveals the difficulties one encounters in deciphering what actually took place. The charming, naive drawings attempt to show in one scene a whole sequence of events as comprehended by the compiler.

The purpose of all the detail was to give the population as much information as possible. It gives us some conception of the type of warfare practiced. The closed-formation "blocks" of fighting men with intervals between the columns and an abundance of flag-like devices in the first rows are characteristic of the time. Defeated units are shown running separately; single men are detectable. The character of the topography is reflected, but the concept of scale is not applicable.

Whether or not contemporary television, radio, and newspaper journalism does a better job of informing the population on military events of significance is arguable.

Warhaffte Relation vnd Abriß/ deß grossen vfürsehnen Einzahls/ von der ChurBayrischen Reichs Armada sampt den darzu gestoßnen Lothrina: vnd Hatzfeldischen Völckern/ in welchem Sie die Frantzöfisch: vnd Weinmarische Armada / so jun vnd vmb der Statt Duttlingen gelegen/ gantz auffgeschlagen vnd an haben/ So geschehen den 24. Novembris, Anno 1643.

FIGURE 8. Charles X Gustav of Sweden (1622-1660).

Charles X was a king with a methodical approach to warfare. His thoughts on the advantage of surprise offered by weather and environment were innovative. If an attack in good weather and during summertime is expected, then why not conduct warfare in the winter? Or, if a water body covered with thin ice is considered impassable, why not reinforce the ice and carefully spread the load in order to arrive unexpectedly? The ideas may appear simple after the fact. But they involved thinking, action and conclusion.

FIGURE 9. Frederick the Great (1712-1786), King of Prussia.

When the situation required, Frederick conducted warfare in the winter, but he did not display any special measures or any special means to use winter to his advantage. He was a colorful figure, full of contrasts and contradictions. Refinements in taste, knowledge of classical music, and a certain liberality went hand-in-hand with harsh military training in a class army. And a sort of coquettishness toward universal rights for everyone before the law went hand-in-hand with the military concept of the worthlessness of soldiers' (in this case peasants') lives on the battlefield if a quick victory could be obtained.

His harsh drilling, discipline, and hardship training were accepted and used in full measure by many followers. It is said that his soldiers were more afraid of their officers than of enemy bullets. Tradition has it that a unit of his tall grenadiers once became panicky and started to run in disorder. The furious king began running around and hitting the soldiers with his walking cane, shouting, "What's the matter with you guys? Do you want to live forever?!" It may have been the truth.

FIGURE 10. Napoleon Bonaparte (Buonaparte), 1769-1821.

Napoleon was a self-made military leader possessed of considerable luck, and a gifted statesman and politician. He was born in Ajaccio, Corsica, of Italian parents, and educated in France. His main talents were in politics. He had a strong personality, and was a gifted military leader as long as his luck lasted. Men enthusiastically gave their lives for him on the battlefield.

Napoleon became the military dictator of France in 1799. In 1802 he was designated "Counsul of France for Life." He became Emperor of France, to discourage further assassination attempts, as Joseph Fouché suggested. The "Napoleonic Era" comprised a series of wars and battles which reshaped completely the political map of Europe. Without first bringing hostilities with England to an end, Napoleon assembled his famous Grande Armée and invaded Russia in 1812. Unprepared, the Russians retreated without fighting the "decisive battle" Napoleon was craving, leaving behind "scorched earth." Napoleon had to press on to Moscow over devastated, guerrilla-infested land until finally the Russians under Count Kutusoff were ready to give battle at Borodino on September 7, 1812. The battle lasted a whole day and was undecisive. After sunset both sides ceased hostilities, mainly due to fatigue and exhaustion. Kutusoff disengaged and Moscow was occupied by the invaders.

The uncertain situation, the inability to provision his army, and the many fires in the city soon made Napoleon decide to withdraw. A short battle south of Moscow forced him to take once more the already devastated Smolensk route. With great loss of men and materiel Napoleon recrossed Russia, reaching the border in November. He had only 12,000 fighting men with him; he had started out with 453,000!

Many serious historical sources hint, indicate or insist that the main reason for Napoleon's retreat was the "harsh Russian winter." The recorded fact is that the winter of 1812-1813 was rather mild and late. We discuss Napoleon here because of that legend about "winter hardship." The fact is that a normal winter would actually have helped him, at least in one instance. In western Russia is the River Berezina, which had to be crossed over rather poor bridges, with great losses of men, horses and cannon. Had there been an average winter there would have been ice on the river, and the losses would have been significantly less.

There is something mysterious about many great leaders, generals, or emperors. A long streak of luck allows them to be recorded in history as great and famous men of genius. But once luck fails them, they begin to act irrationally and incomprehensibly, and lose the ability to extricate themselves from critical situations by energetic leadership. Napoleon abandoned his forces and hurried back to France to meet some other crisis. But his historians never abandoned him — they created a face-saving legend about defeat by snow, ice and frost.

FIGURE 11. The Battlefield of Waterloo.

The map shows the disposition of forces on the morning of June 18, 1815. The subsequent battle, delayed by Napoleon to give the muddy ground a chance to dry, was not an example of tactical innovation. But it was an important historical event — the final defeat of Napoleon. Together with illustrations created by "batalists" (artists specializing in battle scenes) maps of this type constitute important historical material, although they often contain very little useful information. One observation can be made. The general growth of the armies, the ever-increasing use of black powder, and the increasing size of the battlefields made the control and direction of a battle virtually impossible. (Consider that the distance from Plancenoit to Maransart is approximately 3 km.) Therefore, once all the "blocks of people" were engaged, the commander became essentially an observer, with the exception that he could hold back and then engage reserves in places he imagined to be important. New methods of battlefield communication were badly needed. An observer of such an intense battle could not predict its outcome very well until its very end.

There is a curious legend connected with the Battle of Waterloo. It is said that Natan Rothschild (1777-1836) observed the battle, and when the end came he rushed to the coast on fast horses, crossed the channel, and raced to London. He sold his French stock on the London exchange and invested the proceeds in English shares. Because there was no telegraph, Rothschild became one of the richest men in England overnight. The poet Heinrich Heine called him Natan the Wise.

After Waterloo, winter battles were fought with much smaller armies, and improved communications gave the commander the means to command during the battle.

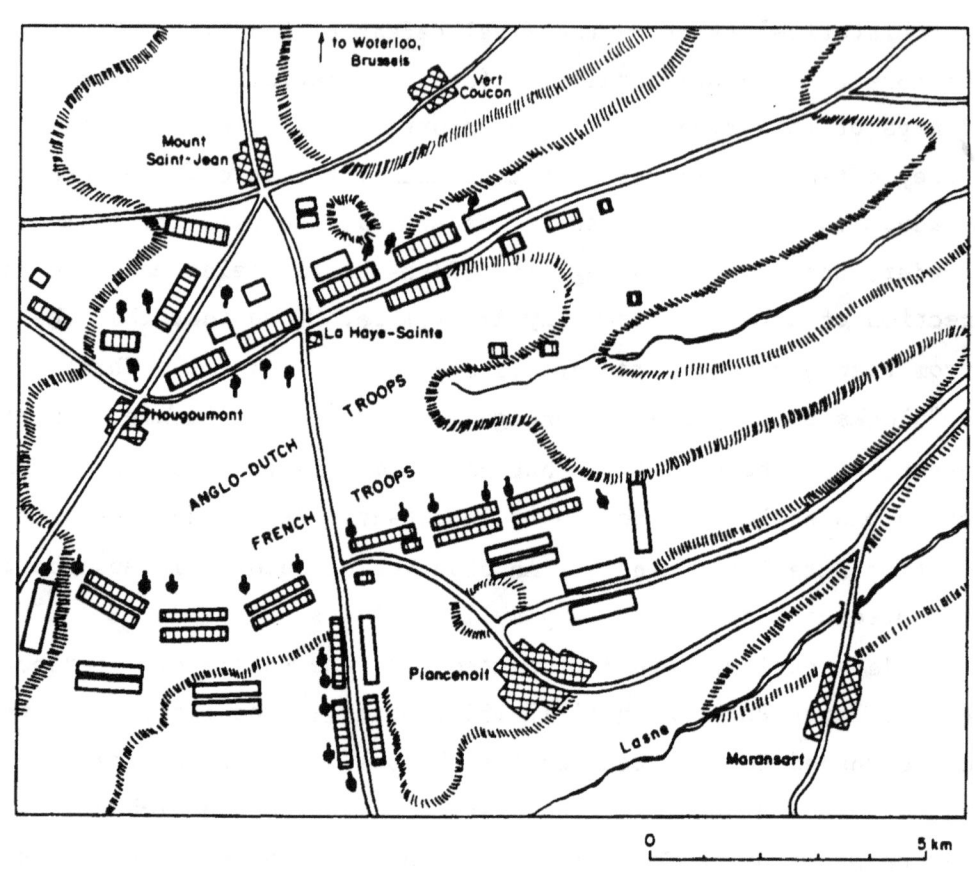

FIGURE 12. Crossing the Balkans in the Russian-Turkish War.

This unique winter operation is considered to have been the most important for the Russians in the whole Turkish campaign of 1877. The Russians occupied the three passes through the Balkans (Konak, Trojan and Shipka), and used the time to gather forces, supplies and ammunition. Then, on 13 December 1877, General Gurko broke out during a blizzard, pushed into the valley, and threatened Sofia, the capital of Bulgaria. Threatened from the flank, the main Turkish forces under Suleiman Pasha gave up the capital. On 23 December, Kartsev's force broke out. Finally, on 28 December, the defensive Turkish positions at the Shipka Pass were overpowered, and Radetsky marched south, threatening the whole Maritsa Valley. This triple flank maneuver destabilized the Turkish forces, which suddenly found themselves without defensible wintertime bases. The march east along the Maritsa River was energetic enough to prevent the Turks from throwing up defensive positions strong enough to shield Constantinople.

The Russians realized that the strategic objective — the Bosphorus Strait and Constantinople — was all but attained. There was no way for the disorganized Turkish army to stem the Russian winter offensive. But then came international politics, diplomacy, threats and treaties. The pens of the diplomats proved more powerful than the Russian bayonets. Russia failed to obtain control over the Bosphorus.

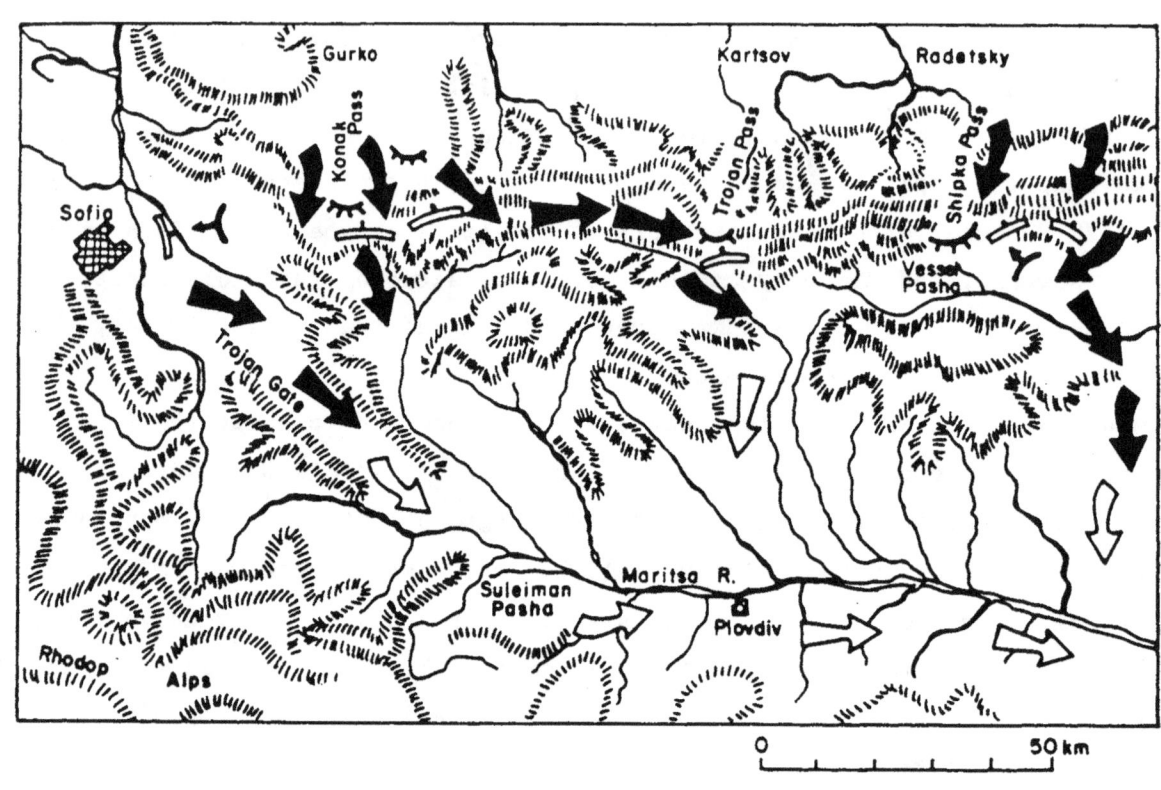

FIGURE 13. Crossing the Shipka Pass.

In the Russian-Turkish war the so-called "Shipka sitting" during the first part of the winter of 1877-1878 (Figure 12) resulted in considerable non-combat losses for the Russians. Nevertheless, disadvantageous as it was, the position had to be held to allow reinforcements and materiel to be brought up. The Turks, under Vessel Pasha, had fortified the pass. Their main forces were in the fortified town of Sheinovo. The Russian assault, coordinated with the other two Balkan crossings, was a flanking maneuver performed in difficult terrain under harsh winter conditions. Radetsky attacked the Turks head-on to attract and hold the Turkish forces, while Sviatopolk-Mirsky with 18,000 men and Skobelev with 16,000 performed difficult flanking marches. Sixteen hours later than planned, Skobelev still surprised the Turks at Sheinovo. When the forces at the left flank occupied the towns of Giussovo, Ianina and Kazanlyk, Vessel Pasha was encircled, and soon capitulated. The Russians lost 5000 killed and wounded against 1000 Turkish casualties during the five-day battle. The Russian army captured 22,000 men, including 765 officers. Thirteen thousand Turks dispersed and slipped away over forest trails.

With the Shipka assault, the Balkan crossing was completed. The Turks in the Maritsa Valley had been outmaneuvered.

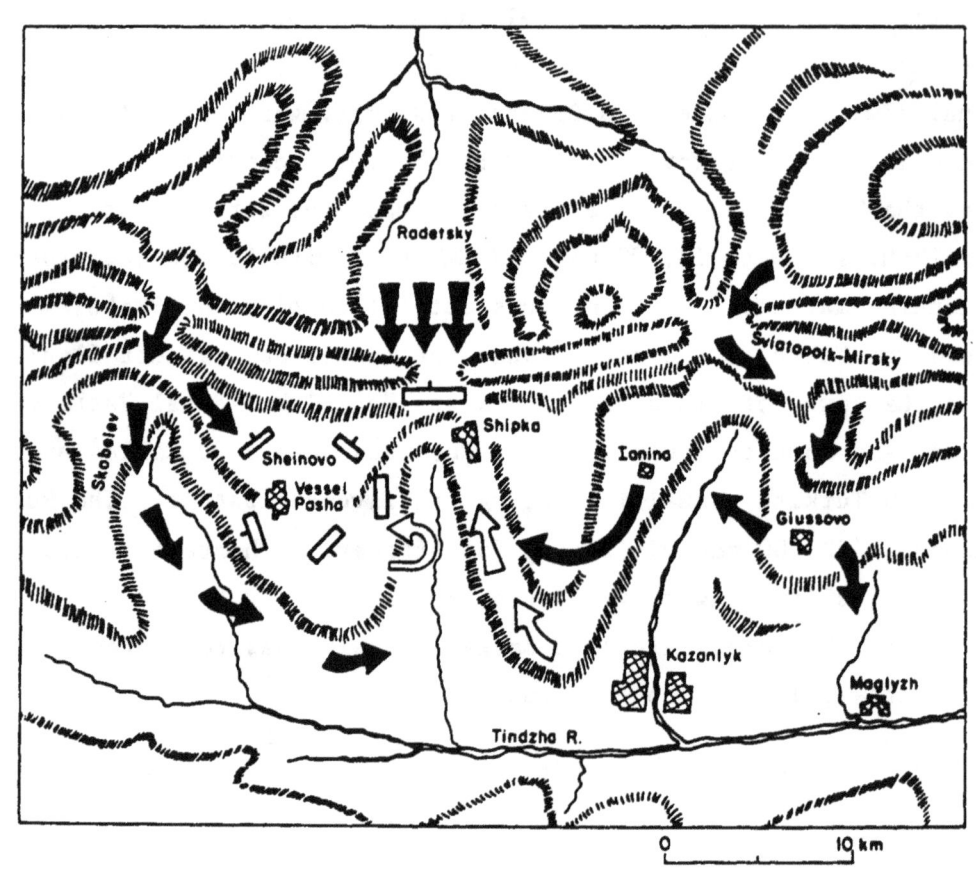

FIGURE 14. Finnish Military Skiers.

Military skiing differs considerably from the civilian winter sport. Its purpose is to enable fighting men to move over otherwise impassable terrain. The speed of ski marches may be considered modest compared with civilian cross-country ski racing, but at the end of a march there is not a finish line but often engagement of the adversary. Furthermore, ski troops carry their weapons, ammunition and life support equipment. The skiers in the Finnish Army are capable of remaining outdoors for prolonged periods without the impairment or loss of their combat capabilities.

The men here wear their duty uniforms and fur hats and are armed. The first man carries an automatic rifle; the second has a light machine gun. In their rucksacks they may have extra underwear, socks, rations and personal hygiene articles. The Finnish Army is trained for marching and bivouacking at any time of the year in any weather.

FIGURE 15. Finnish Jaegers.

In the winter these men travel by bicycle over highways, roads and trails. Off the roads, usually before engaging the adversary, Jaegers move on skis. Russian veterans of the Winter War of 1939-1940 relate that Finnish skiers skillfully used slopes to inflict lightning-fast automatic fire and hand grenade attacks and disappeared before any resistance could be organized. In small unit tactics Jaegers may be compared with mobile units of light cavalry, but with more firepower and without the thunderous noise of cantering horses.

In proper terrain and with suitable tactics the Jaeger can be a formidable fighter. An enemy column on the march can be brought to the point of exhaustion by numerically inferior ski troops. Harassment, and denial of bivouac safety or rest, reduces fighting power and can lead to the complete destruction of a strong adversary, superior in numbers and equipment.

Normally, we are reluctant to use bicycles on snow and ice. But the skill to use a bike on surfaces other than asphalt can be learned fast. Everywhere behind the front lines in a battle area the roads are normally open. The Jaegers may end up at a place other than where their bicycles are — but that is not as important as the accomplishment of the mission.

FIGURE 16. A Squad of Skiers in the Northern Wilderness of Finland.

These men can travel over long distances and can remain independent of supply bases for a relatively long time. The greatest value of the type of training such ski squads have is their ability to make large areas insecure for the adversary, to operate behind the lines, and to engage the enemy where they are not expected. Also, skiers can reach areas nobody else can, except perhaps paratroopers. But once landed, parachute troops need skis too, or they will just sit in the snow.

Finnish infantrymen familiar with cross-country skiing literally since early childhood can move on skis over long distances without losing their combat capability.

FIGURE 17. An Ambush Position.

The men form a Finnish recoilless anti-tank rifle team. They are in white camouflage clothing and are partially buried in snow. There is some question as to whether or not small automatic weapons function properly in snow. Finnish weapons perform well.

FIGURE 18. Carl-Gustav baron Mannerheim (1868-1951), Marshal of Finland.

This popular Finnish statesman and general made an important contribution to the art of winter warfare. Baron Mannerheim participated in five wars — the 1904 Russo-Japanese war, the First World War (in the Russian Imperial Service), the White Finnish Liberation War (1918), the Winter War of 1939-1940, and the Second World War. His tactical innovations made the Finnish Army the most effective winter warfare force in the world. Fundamentally the Finns practiced a mobile, active form of elastic defense mostly conducted by independently acting, self-sufficient units. Flexibility, full utilization of terrain, aggressiveness, and skill were the basic attributes of the Finnish winter warriors. Mannerheim's leadership and command methods were to a great degree opposite to our current practice. He encouraged, supported and demanded initiative, energy and independent action. Giving explicit orders to a field unit from general headquarters, in the way now possible using modern communication methods, was simply unthinkable (see, for example, "Raids and National Command: Mutually Exclusive", by Lt. Col. Peter A. Kelly, Military Review, April 1980).

In international relations Mannerheim had to suffer many bitter disappointments. In the Winter War it was the promised western support that never came (except for a few Scandinavian volunteers). In World War II, England, upon Stalin's insistence, declared war with Finland. Mannerheim could never comprehend the slavish eagerness of western democracies to please and placate Stalin.

FIGURE 19. Stalin (1879-1953).

This revolutionary Marxist-terrorist, whose true name was Iosif Vissarionovich Dzhugashvili, was for the last 25 years of his life the absolute dictator of Russia. He concentrated absolute power in his hands, began the modernization of heavy industry, and conducted the collectivization of agriculture at the cost of 10 million people. Ever since, Russia has been dependent on foreign sources of food.

During Stalin's rule Russian military potential became seriously weakened by a bloody purge among all ranks of command (Alexandrov, 1969). He committed grave errors as supreme commander of all Russian forces during World War II. During the initial stages of German advance there was mass encirclement and extermination of whole armies. Several million fighting men were lost. The pressure from the very top ("Not a step back!" and "Attack at all costs!") resulted in the waste of manpower and resources. Stalin was a poor military strategist.

His greatest achievement was in international politics. During his regime all western powers developed the curious "progressive," subservient attitude of avoiding irritating the Russian leadership at all costs. This attitude has persisted ever since. Credit for that is due to Stalin alone.

Stalin is often given credit for the "inhuman," "bloody," "horrible" purges and exterminations he conducted. The fact is that when a modern absolute dictatorship takes over, certain classes or groups of people lose the privilege of being alive. Purges, terrors, and mass exterminations must take place, and must periodically be repeated. Stalin's predecessor, Lenin (Vladimir Il'ich Ul'ianov), had to conduct extensive purges, and eliminated certain classes of the population. Stalin inherited Lenin's extermination apparatus and improved its functioning. To name another example, the Chinese Revolution and the subsequent Cultural Revolution resulted in a much larger number of people losing their right (privilege) to be alive. While the need to purge and exterminate is clearly recognized by dictators, the particular group or class of people who "need" to be exterminated is sometimes not recognized at the beginning. In such cases race or religion can be reasons for the need to lose life. An example is Adolph Hitler's "effort." It is clear that had Hitler's Germany survived, he would have had to search for and find other categories and classes of people to be exterminated. Otherwise the Eichmanns and Kochs would have had nothing to do. And this would have caused difficulty.

It is debatable which is more "humane" — mass executions or putting people in concentration camps where they are forced to do heavy work and are given little or no of food and shelter. With increasing maturity of a dictatorial system the ratio of mass executions to masses in concentration camps becomes smaller. That is why Southeast Asia is now the scene of primitive mass executions, while Russia has its highly developed concentration camp system.

A historical irony is the fact that a modern dictator cannot control very well the growth of its suppression apparatus (KGB, SS, Gestapo, etc.). That is why the secret power apparatus takes over more and more control functions between the peak purge periods. The secret police in a dictatorship may ultimately take over all the government control functions. But that is irrelevant.

FIGURE 20. George Konstantinovich Zhukov (1896-1974), Marshal of the Soviet Union.

A specialist in command and leadership, Zhukov developed expertise in offensive warfare and was successful in interpreting and implementing Stalin's blanket orders. In military political thinking he advocated independence for the military. In 1941 he was Chief of General Staff. Under his leadership the Russians conducted the first winter offensive. He recognized the role of mobile defense in winter and emphasized the role of artillery in offense and breakthrough. He survived pre- and post-World War II purges, but had a disturbing up and down career. He was a strong believer in quality training and quality equipment.

Zhukov served as an enlisted man in World War I, and was a cavalry officer in the Russian Civil War. In 1941 he was Commander in Chief during the defense of Moscow. Subsequently he commanded and planned most of the major battles of World War II. He prepared and conducted the final assault on Berlin in 1945 and later commanded the occupation forces in East Germany.

Until 1944 his most successful plans were winter operations. Staff work and planning under Zhukov resulted in the Stalingrad encirclement.

FIGURE 21. Preliminary German Plan for the Invasion of Russia in World War II.

In the summer of 1940 the German supreme headquarters envisioned the assault on Russia as a lightning ("blitz") campaign to be conducted in three phases, delineated more or less by the natural boundaries of the great rivers. Three million people, 3000 tanks and 7000 artillery pieces were mobilized in 12 armies divided into three groups. The plan called for the annihilation of most of the Russian forces during the first stage. Most of the resistance was to be over before the end of summer and Phase III. The German Armed Force Economic Division assumed that after Phase III most Russian industrial potential would be in German hands, and the rich agricultural area of the Ukraine would significantly improve Germany's economic base.

The greatest deficiency of the preliminary planning as well as the subsequent "Plan Barbarossa" (see Fig. 22) was the absence of any contingency planning. Most important, the plan assumed only summer operation. As unbelievable as it may sound, the German army had no warm winter clothing and no winterized equipment or materiel. Their equipment was good only for summer.

FIGURE 22. Plan Barbarossa.

This was the WWII campaign plan for a war of annihilation against Russia. The planning took place over a long period, and several versions were produced by the German high command. The Germans considered themselves superior technologically; they had an experienced army and were more efficiently organized. Two factors contributed to their confidence: the Russians made a very poor showing in the Finnish Winter War, and a large number of highly qualified military specialists perished in the great purges.

Initial exploratory staff work began shortly after the French campaign in June 1940, resulting in a strategic survey in October of the same year. Operational planning continued until June 1941. The plan called for all objectives to be reached before the onset of winter. Yet the offensive did not begin until 22 June. At least two months were lost to unexplainable delays. The plan's objective was the collapse of the Communist regime, and it required the annihilation of most of the Russian forces in the western part of Russia, essentially west of the River Dniepr. Also, the Germans counted on the Russian agricultural and industrial production as well as mineral resources and forced labor.

The very first months of the war appeared to proceed according to plan Barbarossa. A strategic surprise was achieved, and the rapidly advancing forces encircled and annihilated large Russian Army groups west of the River Dniepr. The badly equipped, disorganized, and poorly supplied Red Army lost several million men. But the success was illusionary. The German communication lines became overextended over poor highways. Agriculture yielded nothing. And the industrial plant was dismantled and, in a gigantic, ant-like effort, transported across the Urals. What was left behind was destroyed. The only thing the Germans could put their hands on was a large forced labor manpower pool, which was transported to Germany and used in industry and agriculture.

The plan was faulty. There were no provisions made in case the campaign lasted longer than planned. So for the rest of the war the Germans had to improvise, making short-term operational plans and taking emergency measures. Their greatest shortcoming was their failure to plan for a winter campaign and their inability to conduct winter warfare.

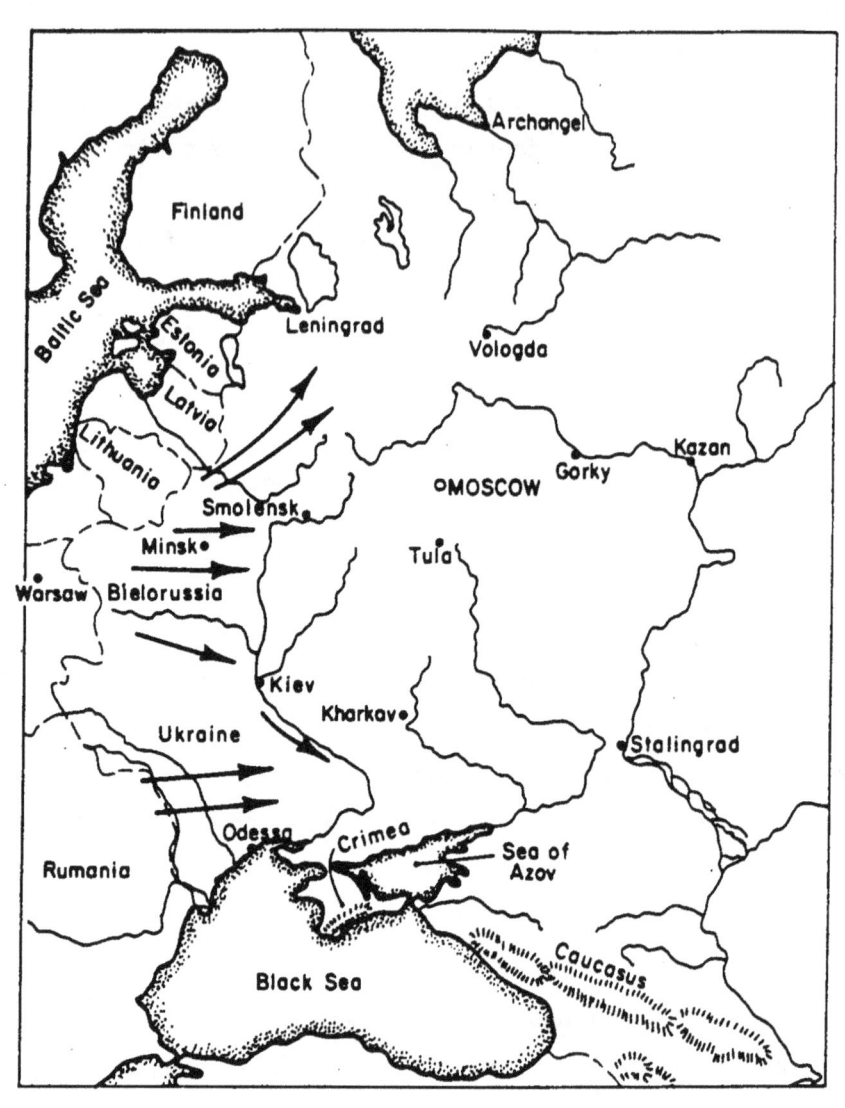

Figure 23. World War II: The Command of the German Forces.

Hitler was not only the Reichskanzler of Germany, he was also the supreme commander of the armed forces. The formal chart does not reflect the depth to which his orders reached in the chain of command. As is often the case when powerful dictators are unchecked by any built-in control mechanisms, Hitler's commands penetrated easily down to very low tactical levels. Reports on situations and conditions sent up the command ladder reached the top only with considerable difficulty. Also, there was a tendency to select and consider situation reports that favored preconceived intentions. That is why during the winter of 1941-1942 reports on unpreparedness, frost injury losses, lack of winter clothing, etc. were not sufficiently considered, and general unpreparedness for winter warfare was taken too late into account.

An action order is contemplated when a need arrises; it is given when the means to implement it are available. The need for an action is determined at the top of the chain of command; the means to implement it are at the bottom. When an order is given without information from the bottom, it may be meaningless or it may be harmful. In the later stages of the war, Hitler was issuing commands to units which no longer existed.

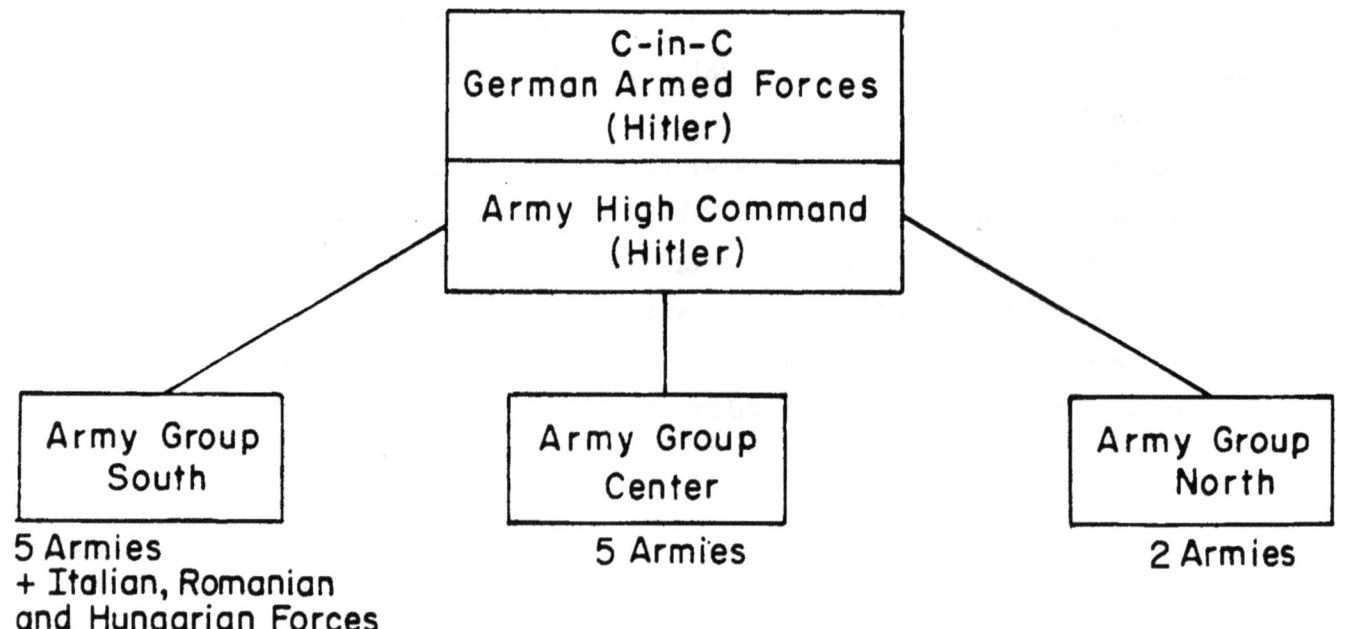

FIGURE 24. World War II: The Battle of Moscow.

The rapid advance of the Germans in 1941 slowed down in the mud of the fall, and they came to a complete stop in full view of Moscow. However, the exhausted, poorly equipped troops of the Russian forward screen were barely holding the adversary. The Germans arrived with 14 tank divisions and 11 infantry divisions. But the long march, extended communications and poor preparation for the winter reduced their capabilities. They began to suffer more frost injuries than combat casualties. Their remaining combat vehicles often failed to start in the cold, and rearward communications were hampered by small mobile Russian ski units. Nevertheless, the situation was dangerous for Moscow. The Germans penetrated the Russian defenses and cut the Moskow-Volga River canal at Iakhroma and Dmitrov. The town of Tula, south of Moscow, was encircled. Moscow was evacuated.

The overall command and planning of the Moscow defense was under Zhukov. A line of defense was prepared, with the city as a center point. It appears now that the Germans would not have had sufficient strength to penetrate the fortified city. In the meantime the Russians assembled 18 fresh divisions with enough materiel and armor to launch a counterattack. Their counteroffensive constituted a blow to German morale and confidence from which they never fully recovered. The Germans began to pay tribute to Russian winter warfare skills.

It is said that at one point the availability of three or four fresh divisions would have allowed the Germans to take Moscow. But, like Napoleon, what would they have done with it?

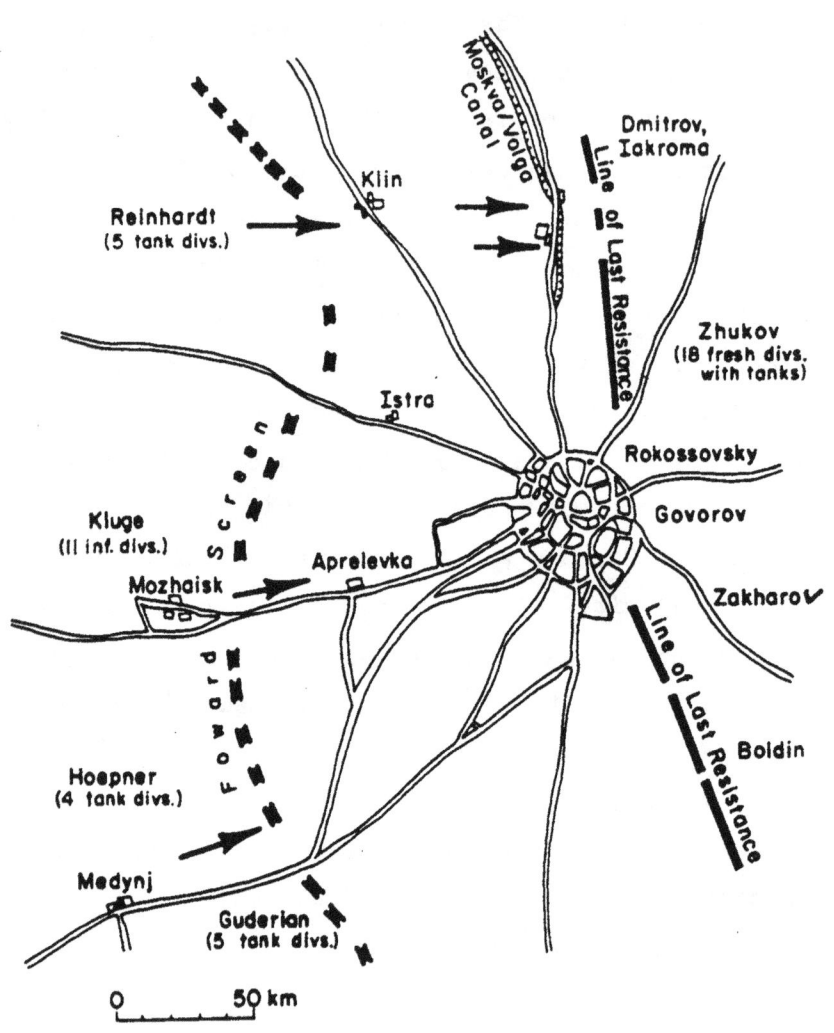

FIGURE 25. World War II: Stalingrad.

This city, stretching 22 miles along the frozen River Volga, was an important industrial center and had extensive shore facilities for freight handling during the navigation season. German forces, including some Rumanian and Italian units, attacked the city from the west, and in a series of bloody battles pushed through to the river. But the city was never entirely cleaned up. The Russian forces defended every building and continued resistance even after being cut in half. The fierce house-to-house combat was equally costly to both sides.

It is not clear why either side was so eager to control this ruined city. There may have been no valid strategic objective, only the city's name. General Erich Paulus, the Commander of the German 6th Army, was given the objective of reaching the Volga and cutting it off. He achieved it. But it was useless; the river was frozen. General Chuikov implemented Stalin's bloody orders — "Not a step back!" — which resulted in enormous losses.

Paulus would have been better off not entering the city. Chuikov would have done better to withdraw from the city and join the forces which later encircled Paulus. The Germans must have been aware of the six armies accumulating north and south, yet they forced themselves into the Stalingrad cauldron.

The situation of the German, Rumanian and Italian forces deteriorated rapidly after encirclement. They lost the airstrip at Kalach, and combat air support became ineffective. Still poorly equipped for winter combat, they suffered from cold and exposure. There were many frost casualties and many wounded soldiers froze to death.

Shortly after encirclement there were realistic chances for Paulus to break out with the help of an outside relief thrust. But Hitler hesitated to give the order. He acted as if he was reluctant to give up Stalingrad. When the order was given it was too late. Von Manstein was dispatched with an armored relief column but it performed poorly in the snow-covered terrain. He was stopped "by infantry combat methods" before reaching the Stalingrad encirclement. Stalingrad was retaken by the Russians. It cost the Germans 250,000 men. Paulus and 23 other captured general officers were used for propaganda purposes.

It is curious that within one person's lifespan this city has been known by three names. Originally it was Tsaritsyn (Queen City); then it became Stalingrad (Stalin City); now it is Volgograd (Volga City). What is there in a city's name to kill people for?

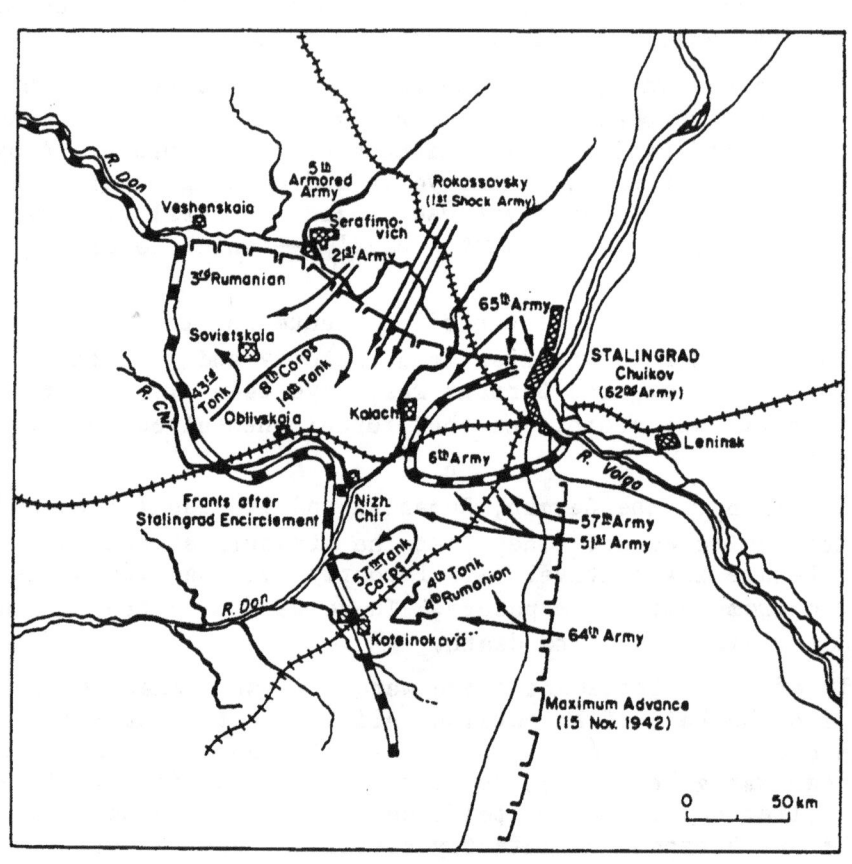

FIGURE 26. A Snow Shelter.

The illustration shows a snow shelter designed according to good European and North American literary traditions. "Igloo" means "house" in Inuit (Eskimo). Many such igloos have been built upon request, according to western specifications, but nobody ever lived in one. When there is a need, and material is available in the form of a large drift of dense, aged snow, Eskimos can build a snow shelter very fast and efficiently. The only two realistic elements in the drawings are the elevated sitting and sleeping platform and the elongated entry tunnel. With the entry plugged, and a cooking fire such as a Primus stove going, the temperature at and above platform level may become quite comfortable. Eskimo women are quite skillful at maintaining a proper combination of heat generation and ventilation by means of a hole poked in the ceiling.

Snow shelters, of any space-conserving shape, can be prepared expeditiously, are warm and healthy, and can be of great benefit, if the two principal features of an access tunnel and an elevated platform are incorporated. But in actuality Eskimos do not particularly care about giving the igloo a neat circular shape.

The National Ski Patrol System, Inc., in its Ski Mountaineering Manual (1980), presents excellent instructions for the construction of snow shelters.

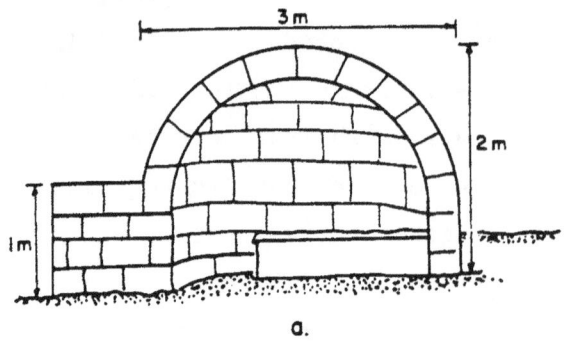

a.

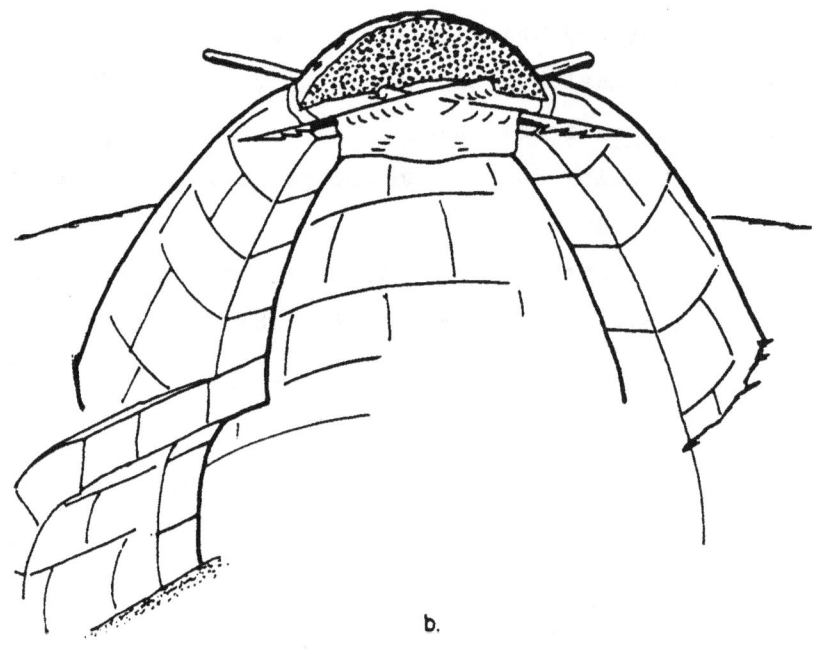

b.

FIGURE 27. Battlefield Locomotion.

A moderately trained man can cover 10 km in 1 hour running or jogging. If he is armed and carrying some ammunition, he will be under considerable strain, and rest may be required. Marching cross-country with intermittent brief rests he can cover 50-60 km/day, even if there is 10-15 cm of snow on the ground. Skiers can march up to 100 km a day over moderately difficult terrain covered with any amount of aged snow, of approximately 0.3 g/cm^3 density. Over light snow, the going becomes slower. Snowshoeing is much harder and slower, but allows men to move where nothing else can. On foot, men are immobilized by little more than 35 cm of snow.

Experiments indicate that an 85-kg man in winter boots sinks only 10 cm into 0.2-g/cm^3 snow. Placing such a load on 0.2-g/cm^3 snow does indeed result in surface collapse and formation of a densified "bubble" under the plate (boot) supporting the load that prevents it from sinking to the bottom of the layer. But men do not stand on one foot very long, and their movement results in sideslip of the pressure bubble. In this way, one sinks almost to the bottom of the snow cover. Dissecting footprints in deep snow made with boots with dirty soles can show the mechanism of foot locomotion in snow.

Most wheeled and track-laying vehicles move <u>through</u> the snow, and a few tens of centimeters immobilizes them. The process is complex. Engineers studying cross-country locomotion must consider many factors, such as ground pressure, snow depth, snow cohesiveness and density, type of under-snow surface, slope, and many others. Sending fighting vehicles onto a snow-covered battlefield may be a serious problem. Terrain covered by 40-50 cm of snow belongs to the skier. Ski troop performance may vary considerably, but so also do conditions of urgency and need.

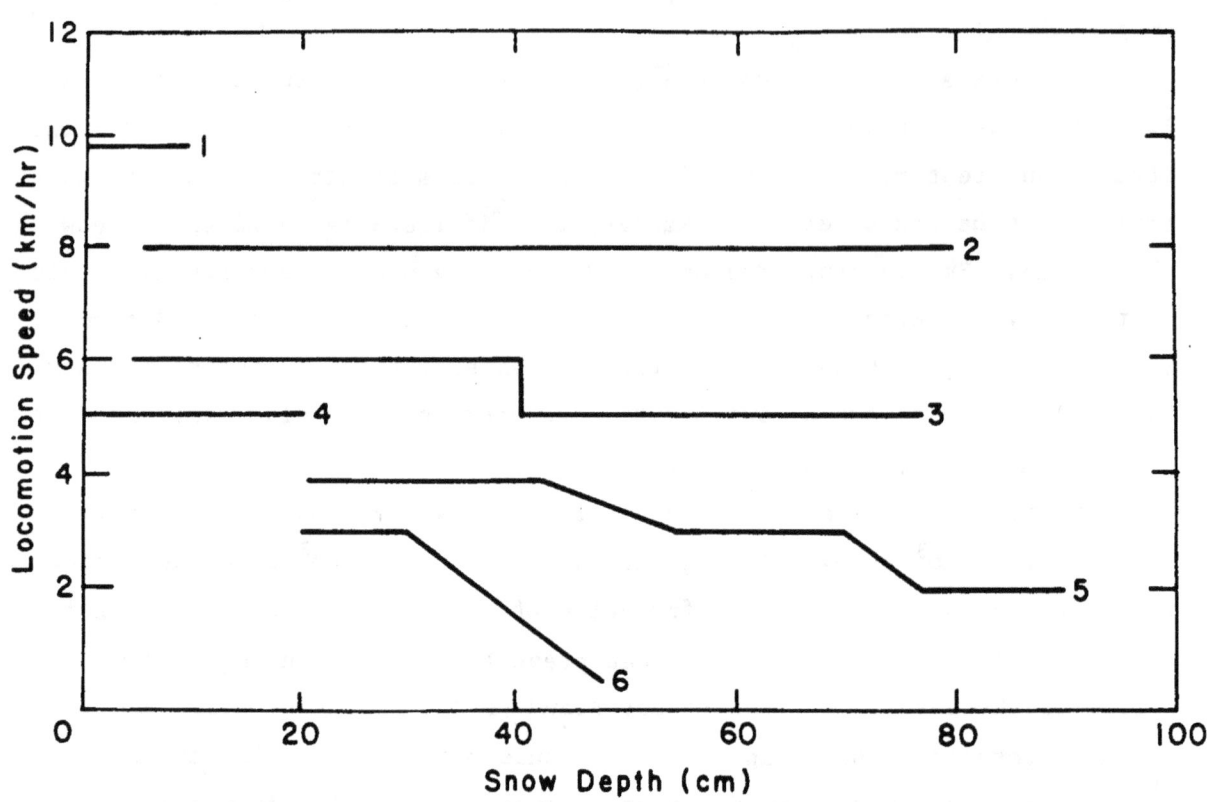

1: Running or jogging (1 hour)
2: Sustained skiing in aged snow
3: Sustained skiing in light snow
4: Marching on foot in up to 20 cm of snow
5: Marching on snowshoes in light snow
6: Marching on foot in more than 20 cm of snow (2 hours)

FIGURE 28. Digging-in.

Two not-very-well conceived facts about a snow cover must be kept in mind. Compared with any type of soil, snow is "labor effective," that is, it can be excavated very fast. The other fact is that snow attenuates fast-moving fragments and small arms projectiles. By piling up snow, or by digging into deeper drifts, roadside berms, etc., a soldier can protect himself from enemy fire very effectively.

At low temperatures a snow cover may have very little cohesion. A vertical snow wall may need conventional sandbags or snow blocks for support. But we find that large feed bags filled with snow are more effective. An aboveground fire position such as is shown here built with snow blocks or large bags is very effective and may be constructed seven to ten times faster than a conventional sandbag structure would be in the summer.

The effect of **any** ammunition is severely degraded by snow. The radius of fragmentation action of a bursting mortar round, for example, can easily be 70% less if it is fired into a surface covered by as little as 35 cm of snow. Only the first round may find the men above the snow surface; they will be within the snow cover when subsequent rounds arrive. Thus the effect of explosive fragmentation ammunition may be severely degraded.

FIGURE 29. Trenches in Snow.

    These are conceptual cross sections from some Russian manuals. The dimensions are in centimeters. It is obvious that such structures have a dual purpose: to protect against aimed fire, and to conceal the movement of individuals and groups of soldiers. In the case of open trenches there are no vertical dimensions given. It is clear that the structures depend upon the depth of the snow cover, as well as its physical properties. Our experience tells us that the excavation of such trenches is labor-effective. It is more than an order of magnitude easier to excavate in snow than in the lightest unfrozen soil. We have found also that there is no need to slant the walls of the trench. The average snow makes stable vertical walls. The two covered trenches were also tried. We found that, as shown, they could be constructed only on paper!

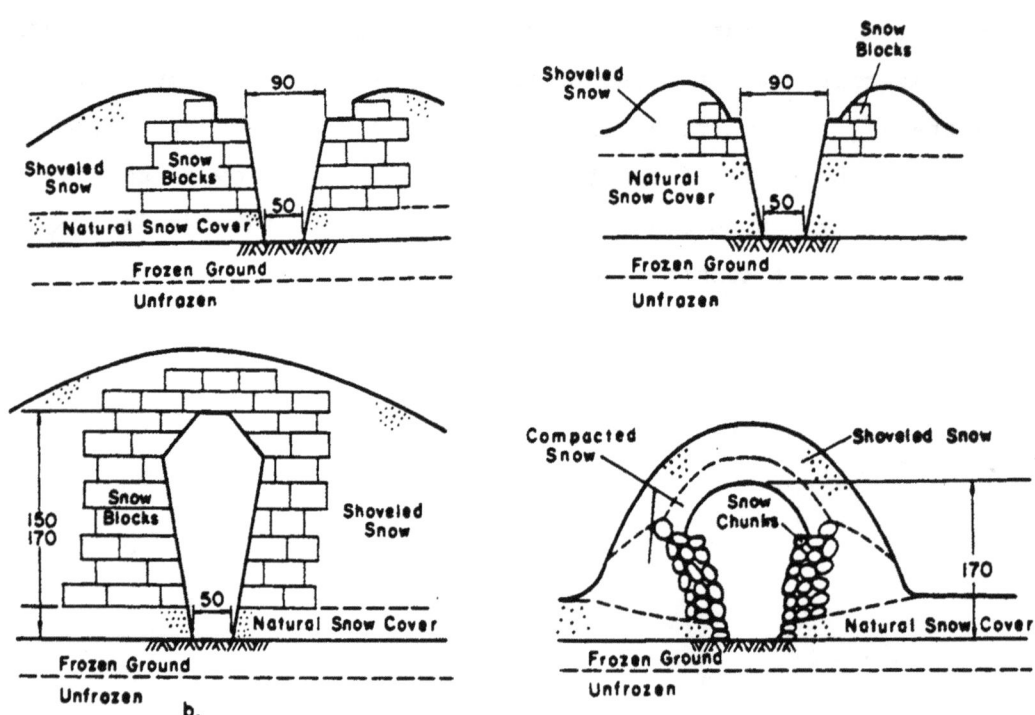

SNOW COMBAT TRENCHES
Dimensions in Centimeters

FIGURE 30. Tank Traps in Snow.

Tank mobility deteriorates rapidly with increasing snow depth. In deep snow tanks slow down and may be stopped completely. The loss of uphill mobility of tanks due to a snow cover is serious.

The drawings, inspired by a Russian training manual, recommend relatively easy ways to increase the difficulties for tanks in snow-covered terrain. Mechanical means of snow moving may provide rapidly constructed tank obstacles.

We discovered also that any flat trajectory fire aimed at tanks behind such snow berms is quite ineffective. The berms provides good protection for tanks.

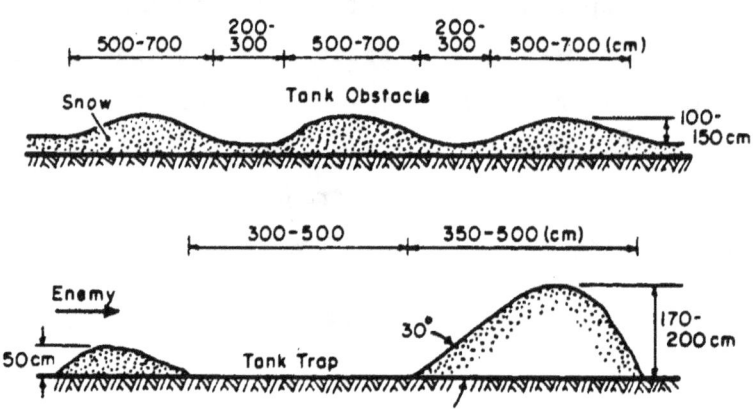

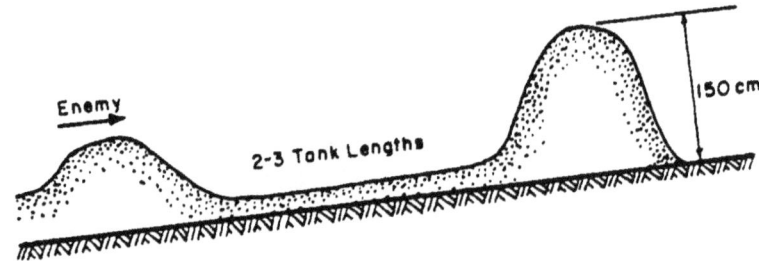

Icing and Steeping of Slope

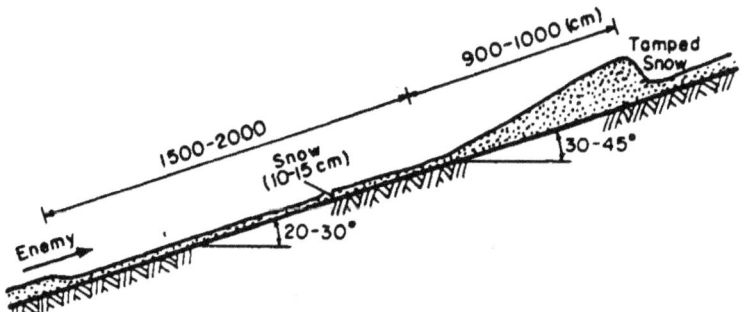

FIGURE 31. Preparing a Covered Trench.

Once it is covered, a trench blends into the landscape, protects against shrapnel, and renders traffic undetectable by hostile observers. The drawing, from a Russian manual, suggests that a movable arch be placed over a snow trench on blocks. The arch is covered with snow, and when (or perhaps if) the snow hardens the arch is moved, blocked up again, etc. We have never tried the procedure, but it appears that during a thaw the snow could be packed and molded around the device very fast. During below-freezing weather, however, one would have to wait several hours before the snow acquired sufficient cohesion to stand up unsupported. There might be a few instances when that would be practicable. Adherence of wet or dry snow to the mold might not be a problem - any oil or grease would help.

Deposited snow differs in density, "hardness," and particle size. Shoveling very light snow from one place to another results in a significant increase in density. The density of snow is expressed in fractions of a gram per cubic centimeter or fractions of a metric ton per cubic meter. Water is approximately 1 g/cm^3; light snow is 0.1 to 0.2 g/cm^3.

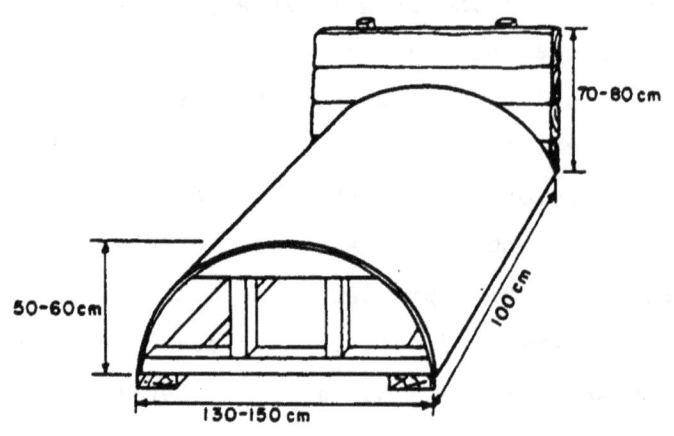

FIGURE 32. Snow Cover Distribution and Duration.

There is a need for much improvement, compilation and reexamination of snow data on a global scale. Much is known for particular areas. For example, winter sports regions have a fairly good conception of depth and duration of snow cover. On a broader scale, the Northern Hemisphere of our planet develops yearly a snow cover which lasts from less than 1 month to 8 or more months at high latitudes. The extremes are warm climates without known snow deposits on the ground and northern ice caps with a permanent, yearly replenished snow cover. Does this mean that the farther north you go the deeper the snow cover is? No.

Does a deeper snow cover last longer? Also no. A snow cover is a function of intricate climatic interrelations. For example, in polar deserts and semideserts there is very little precipitation. If snow is deposited as a blanket during calm weather, which is rare, it may disappear very quickly in the spring. Drifts behind obstacles, especially if shaded from the sun, may survive a long time, sometimes into the following winter.

The map shows snow regions in very broad terms. Very interesting, and therefore intensively recorded and studied, are local deviations from what is shown on the map.

In certain mountain regions spectacular avalanches occasionally bury villages, highways, and skiers (who should know better). In some foothills Foehns, Chinooks and Boras precipitate fantastic thaws and wet snow deposits. At the southern edges of the snow regions snow on the ground may not be experienced for several winters, yet at other times a snow cover may form several times during one winter, disrupting traffic and the pattern of daily life. Catastrophic avalanches, snowstorms and thaws are simply regular phenomena with a low frequency of reappearance.

Most of the industry and population of the Northern Hemisphere is in areas with snowy winters. In the Southern Hemisphere snow does not play such a significant role in man's life. The lines on the map indicate the approximate duration of snow cover during one winter. Very special regions are the permanent ice caps and the Himalayan-Tibetan area, with a permanent snow cover in the former and cool, arid winters and varied snow cover in the latter.

Snow cover on a world-wide scale and its reappearance each winter are still awaiting comprehensive study. Until such a study is performed a military planner must prepare for the worst case.

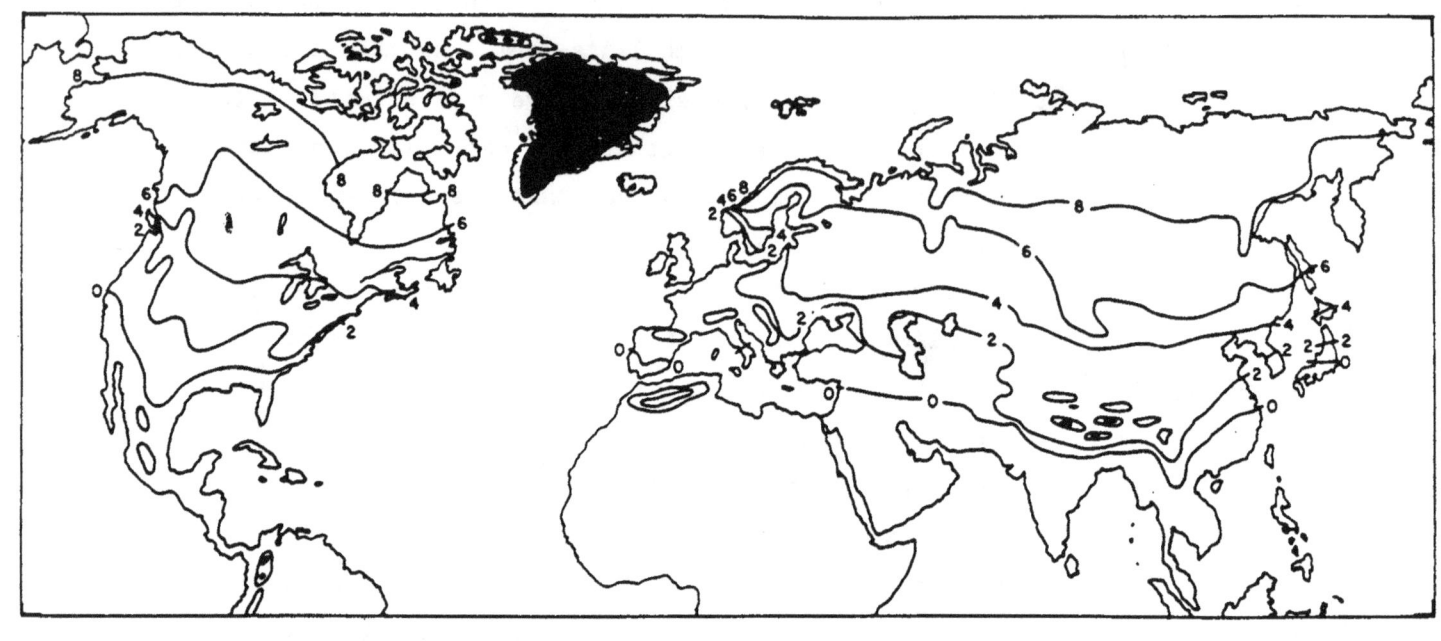

FIGURE 33. Snow Cover Formation.

How does a snow cover form? It is not always simple. A snow cover may fail to form, or it may be unusually persistent, or deep, or variable. But some things about a snow cover may be said with certainty. Provided the temperature is below freezing, it forms a deposit whose thickness depends upon precipitation intensity. Immediately after precipitation snow begins to settle. Subsequent snowstorms add to the depth of a snow cover, and thaw periods may partially or fully destroy it. In our diagram, a. shows a time-depth history for a place with a winter lasting from November until mid April with a January thaw. Figure b. shows a drier, shorter winter without the evidence of a mid-winter thaw. Both diagrams are hypothetical. In practice there is variability from place to place and from one season to the other. There is enough evidence for many places to construct a most probable, or worst case, diagram of snow cover. Diagram c. is entirely hypothetical and sketchy. There are simply not enough data found. But it shows that in the far north a snow cover may not last very long: less snow, faster thaw. Also, if it forms in the south at all it does not last: too warm. The probability of a snowstorm for a military leader is not very important; he counts on the worst case.

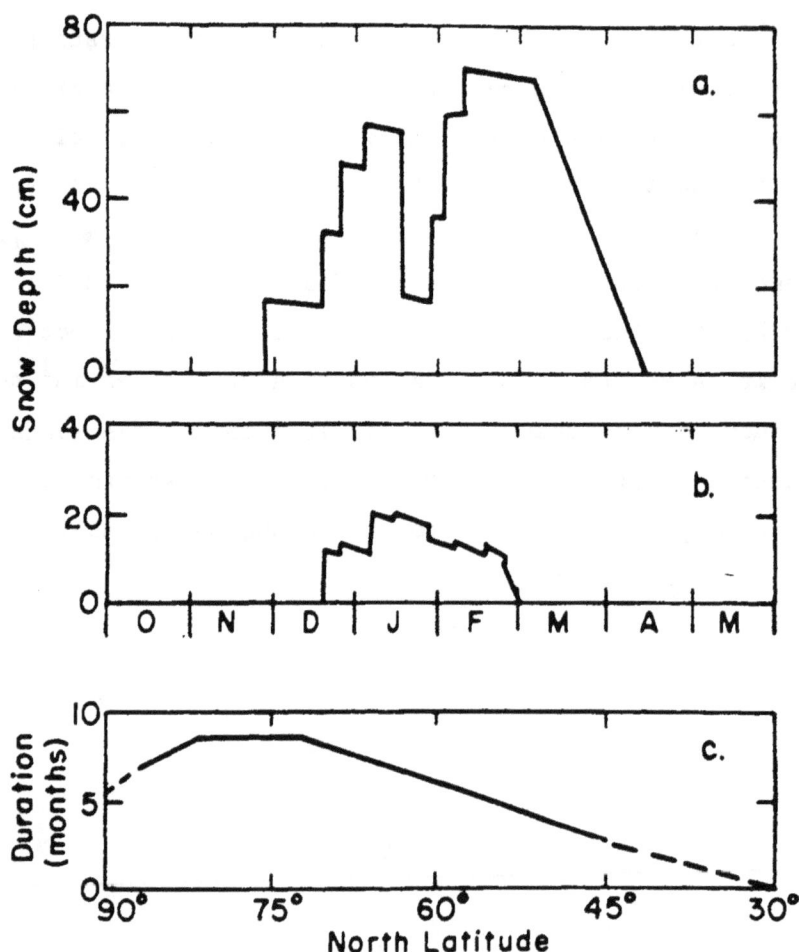

FIGURE 34. Snow Penetration by Fragments.

We took blocks of dense (0.42-g/cm^3) snow and accelerated 5.5-mm metal cubes into it. The snow was sifted through a screen to make it homogeneous. The density was approximately that found in a roadside berm, in a drift, or in a shoveled snow pile. We found that beginning approximately at a velocity of 800 m/s, fragments, simulated by the 5.5-mm cubes, started to deform, and the penetration distance actually declined with further increase in velocity. We found it remarkable that both steel and aluminum began to deform at the same terminal velocity. Only the degree of distortion was different. On another occasion we observed that M-16 rifle ammunition was also deformed when it penetrated a snow target. Automatic point-blank fire aimed at one spot "excavated" a snow target, resulting in a tunnel 1.4 m long. A snow berm 1.5 m deep protects against fragments and small arms fire.

High explosive antitank ammunition (HEAT) with shaped charge action is ineffective if the target is protected by as little as 0.75 m of shoveled snow.

We are now studying the relation of a snow cover and mines and minefields. We may safely say that surprises are expected.

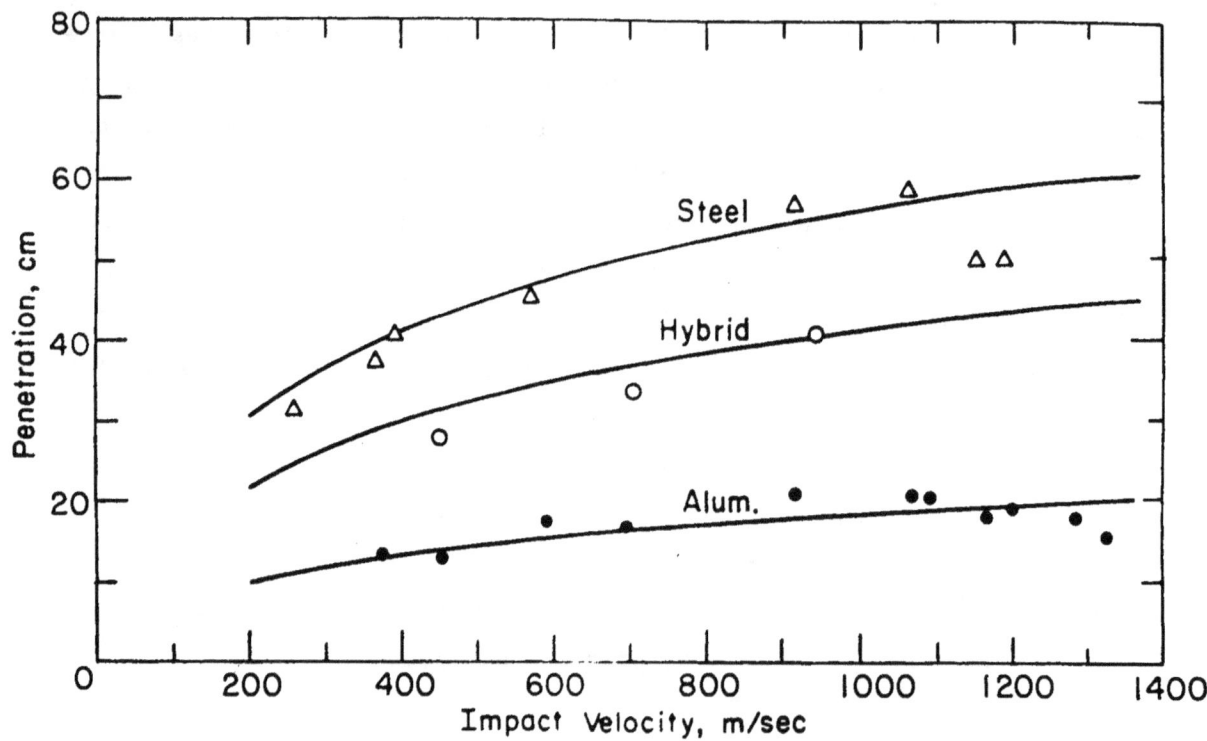

LITERATURE QUOTED

The examined literature contains historical books of either a general or specific nature. Other documents provide instruction in winter warfare techniques. Individual works are indicated by author, date, title and publisher. Periodicals are so marked. The examination of many events required information from foreign sources. Whenever it was practical the title was transliterated, with the translation given in parentheses.

Whenever an original and its translation were available, the former was preferred. In a few important cases a translated source is appended.

Alexandrov, V. (1964) The Tukhachevsky Affair. Prentice Hall, Englewood Cliffs, N.J.

Amosov, S. (1935) Deistvia tankovogo bataliona zimoi (Tank battalion in winter operation). Krasnaia Zvezda (periodical), No. 52, March.

Anonymous (1941) Winterliche Tarnung (Winter Camouflage). In "Kriegskunst in Wort und Bild." Periodical training publication 18. (This useful training material appears in West Germany under the auspices of the Defense Ministry.)

Anonymous (1947) Winter Campaign 1941-1942. Department of the Army. Draft Translation, U.S. Army Office of the Chief Historian, Manuscript D - 184.

Anonymous (1950) The Motti tactics. The Infantry Journal, No. 1.

Assman, Admiral Kurt (1950) The Battle of Moscow - Turning point of the war. Foreign Affairs, Vol. 28.

Avtorkhanov, A. (1973) The Origin of the Partocraty (in two volumes). Possev Verlag (publisher), Frankfurt.

Bader, Henri and Daisuke Kuroiwa (1962) The Physics and Mechanics of Snow as a Material. U.S. Army Cold Regions Research and Engineering Laboratory, Monograph II-B.

Bates, R.E. and M.A. Bilello (1966) Defining Cold Regions. U.S. Army Cold Regions Research and Engineering Laboratory, Technical Report 178.

Belokon', A.P. and V.T. Korneichuk (1964) Inzhenernoie obespechenie nastupleninia motostrelkovogo (tankovogo) batal'ona (roty) [Engineer support for the attack of a motorized (tank) battalion (company)]. Voienizdat, (Ministry of Defense) Moscow.

Biblioteka Ofitsera (1966) Taktika (Tactics). (An instruction series on various aspects of martial art.) Voienizdat (publisher), Moscow.

Blau, E.G. (1955) The German Campaign in Russia - Planning and Operations (1940-1942). Historical Study of the Department of the Army, D.A. Pamphlet No. 20-2610a.

Boltin, E. (1957) Pobeda Sovetskoi Armii pod Moskvoi v 1941 (The victory of the Soviet Army before Moscow in 1941). Voprosy Istorii (periodical), No. 1, 1957.

Bukovsky, W. (1977) Soviet strategy - Russian strategy. International Defense Review (periodical), No. 6.

Carlyle, T. (1899) Frederick the Great. Standard, Boston.

Chekotillo, A.M. (1943) Primenenie Snega L'da i Merzlogo Grunta v Fortifikatsii (The Use of Snow, Ice and Frozen Ground in Fortification). Voienizdat, Moscow.

Clark, A. (1965) Barbarossa. William Morrow and Co., New York.

Clausewitz, von, Carl (1832) Vom Kreige (On War). Note: This important work appeared in many publications and editions. In 1953 there was an edition with unauthorized changes in it — historically unacceptable, as one authority stated. A good English edition is: Rutledge & Keagan Paul, Inc., London, 1940.

Colliander, S.W. (1954) Russian ski patrols action. Befael (international periodical), Vol. 37, No. 1, p. 22.

Conquest, R. (1969) The Great Terror. The MacMillan Company, London.

Corotneff, N. (1943) Red army tanks in winter. Cavalry Journal (periodical), Vol. 52, No. 1.

Dallin, A. (1957) The German Rule in Russia. Collins & Company, London.

Degen, H. (1948) Dreieinhalb Jahre Polarkreig (Three and One Half Years of Polar War). Office, Chief of Military History, Ms. D-337.

Deghtiarev, Col. I.A. (1961) Voienniye Deistvia Zimoi (Winter Operations). Voienizdat, Moscow.

Department of the Army (1950) Russian Combat Methods in World War II. Historical Study, D.A. Pamphlet 20-230.

Department of the Army (1951) Rear Area Security in Russia. Historical Study, D.A. Pamphlet 20-240.

Department of the Army (1953) Small Unit Action During the German Campaign in Russia. Historical Study, D.A. Pamphlet 20-269.

Dodge, T.A. (1895) Gustavus Adolphus. Houghton, Mifflin & Co., New York-Boston.

Dodge, T.A. (1904) Napoleon (Volume III). Houghton, Mifflin & Co., New York-Boston.

Dwinger, E.E. (1943) Wiederseen mit Soviet Russland (Return to Soviet Russia). Stillzegan Verlag, Jena.

Engels, F. (1957) Selected Military Writings. (A Russian collection of translated periodical articles.) Voienizdat, Moscow.

Erfurth, W. (1950) Der Finnische Krieg (1941-1944) [The Finnish War (1941-1944)]. Limes Verlag, Wiesbaden.

Erfurth, W. (1951) Warfare in the Far North. D.A. Pamphlet 20-292.

Fainshmidt, Ia. D. (1967) Polezniye Sovety Voinu (Useful Advice for the Warrior). Voienizdat, Moscow.

Firsoff, V.A. (1943) Ski Track on the Battlefield. H.S. Barnes & Co., New York.

Fletcher, C.R.L. (1892) Gustavus Adolphus. MacMillan and Company, London.

Frashe, R.M. (Major) (1976) The Soviet Motorized Rifle Company. Defense Intelligence Agency, Reproduction DD-1-1100-77-76.

Gavrichkov, A. (1929) Opyt Rascheta Skorosti Dvizhenia na Lyzhakh (Calculation of Ski Travel Time). Voennyi Vestnik (periodical), Vol. 9, No. 1, January.

Gilbert, F. (1950) Hitler Directs his War. University of Pennsylvania Historical Archives; also microfilms of Hitler conferences, Library of Congress.

Gindley, A. (1884) The Thirty Year War. Putnam's Sons Publishing House, New York.

Grouzdev, N.I. (1944) Tanki (Tanks), Gosmashinizdat (publisher), Moscow.

Guderian, H. (1952) Errinerungen eines Soldaten (A Soldier's Memories). Vowinkel Verlag, Heidelberg.

Gurevich, M.M. and A. Pucheiko (1945) Printsipy Voiennoi Opticheskoi Maskirovki i Demaskirovki (Principles of Military Camouflage and Decamouflage). USSR Academy of Science, Moscow.

Heidenstam, V.V. (1925) The Swedes and their Chieftans. Oxford University Press, London.

Hersetsky, von, A. (1909) The Chief Campaigns in Europe since 1792. John Murray Co. Publ. Est., London.

Hesse, E. (1969) Der Sovietrussische Partisanenkrieg (1941-1944) im Spiegel Deutscher Kampfamweisungen and Befehle (The Soviet Guerrilla War 1941-1944, Reflected in German Combat Advisories and Orders), Musterschmidt, Frankfurt.

Howarth, H.R. (1876) History of the Mongols. Longmans Green & Co., London.

Institut Marksizma-Leninizma (1964) Istoria Velikoi Otechestvennoi Voiny Sovetskogo Soiuza (1941-1945) [History of the Soviet Union's Great Patriotic War (1941-1945)]. Partizdat (or Politizdat?), Moscow.

Jacks, L.V. (1930) Xenophon, Soldier of Fortune. C. Scribner Sons, New York.

Jarrinen, Y.A. (1944) Finnish and Russian Tactics in the Winter War. Werner Söderström, D.Y. (WSOY) (publisher), Helsinki.

Johnson, P.R. (1977) Defensive Works of Subarctic Snow. U.S. Army Cold Regions Research and Engineering Laboratory, CRREL Report 77-6.

Karatun, F.I. (1940) Ukreplenie Mestnosti Zimoi (Terrain Fortification in Winter). Voienizdat, Moscow.

Khrushchev, N.A. (1954) The Dethronement of Stalin. Manchester Guardian. Text reprint. This speech of high political interest may also be obtained from Rafael (publ.), Munich, 1958, under the title: Theme speech on the closed session of the XX CPSU Congress (35 pp). Interesting is Khrushchev's (1961) closing speech at the XXII CPSU Congress as reflected in stenographic procedures, Volume II, p. 651 and subsequent, published in Russian by Partizdat, Moscow. Otherwise, there are many abbreviated versions of pertinent parts of the speeches in circulation.

Kissinger, H.A. (1957) Nuclear Weapons and Foreign Policy. Harper & Bros., New York.

Kliuchevsky, V.O. (1904) Istoria Rossiiskogo Gosudarstva (History of Russia), Vol. I. A.V. Marks, Moscow.

Knizhnikov, L. (1937) Tankovyi Vzvod v Nastuplenii Zimoi .(Winter Attack of a Tank Platoon). Avtobronetankovyi Zhurnal (periodical), Vol. 7, No. 3, p. 8.

Koeppen, W. (1918) Klassifikation der Klima nach Temperatur, Niederschlag und Jahreslauf (Climate Classification by Temperature, Precipitation and Season). Peterman's Mitteilungen (semiperiodical), Berlin - Leipzig.

Kuz'min, P.P. (1957) Fizicheskie svoistva snezhnogo pokrova (Physical Properties of Snow Cover), Gidrometizdat, Leningrad.

Lechens, W. (1959) Der Kampf des Panzers im Winter (Tank Battle in Winter). Wehrausbildung in Wort and Bild; 2-12. (This training periodical appears under the West German Defense Ministry)

Ljungner, A. (1955) Fighting in Deep Snow. Befael, Munchen 38 (1).

Liddel-Hart, H. (1950) Was Russia close to defeat? Military Review, Vol. 30, No. 4 (July).

Limno, A. (1973) V usloviakh snezhnykh zanosov (Under snow drift conditions). Voiennyi Vestnik (periodical) No. 12, December.

Lomov, N. (Col.) (1965) The Influence of Soviet Military Doctrine on the Development of Military Art. Communist of the Military Forces (Periodicals), Moscow, November 1965. (Microfilm can be seen in the New York Public Library.)

Lysukhin, I.F. (Col.) (1968) Inzhenernoie obespechenie forsirovania rek (Engineering requirements in river crossing), Voiennoie Izdatel'stvo, Moscow.

Magidoff, R. (1953) The Kremlin vs. the People. Doubleday, New York.

Mannerheim, C.G. (Marshall) (1952) Errinerungen (Memories). Atlantis Verlag, Zurich.

Mao Tse-Tung (1953) Selected Works (in Russian). Mysl' Publishing House (from the Kharbin Chinese edition).

Matsulenko, V. (1968) Razvitie taktiki nastupatel'nogo boia (The development of offense tactics), Voienno - Istoritsheskii Zurnal (periodical) No. 2, February.

Mellor, M. (1964) Properties of Snow. U.S. Army Cold Regions Research and Engineering Laboratory, Monograph III-A1.

Meyerhofer, A. (1949) Finsk och Rysk vintertaktik (Finnish and Russian winter tactics). Ny Militaer Tidskrift (periodical), No. 22.

Military Historical Commission (1913) Description of the Russian-Turkish War on the Balkan Peninsula, 1877-1878. Official Publication of the Supreme Headquarters, St. Petersburg, 9 volumes.

M.K. (1938) Protivotankovyie prepiatstvia v zimnikh usloviakh (Winter anti-tank barriers). Voiennyi Vestnik (periodicals), Vol. 18, No. 1, p. 46.

Montross, L. (1944) War Through the Ages. Harper and Brothers, New York.

Moore, J.R (1920) American Expedition Fighting the Bolsheviki. The Polar Bear Publishing Company, Detroit.

Munzel, O. (Maj. Gen.) (1949) Tactical and Technical Specialties of Winter Warfare. U.S. Army European Command, Headquarters Historical Division, Manuscript No. p-089.

Nemirovich-Danchenko, V.P. (1879) A Year of War (war correspondent's diaries), 2 volumes. St. Petersburg Publ. (official).

Philippi, A. and F. Heim (1962) Feldzug Gegen Soviet Russland (Campaign Against Soviet Russia). Stuttgart.

Phillips, T.R. (1940) Roots of Strategy. Military Service Publishing Co., Harrisburg, Pennsylvania.

Platonov, S.F. (1910) History of Russia. A.V. Marks, Moscow. English translation: MacMillan, New York, 1925.

Pospelov, P.N. (ed.) (1965) The Great Patriotic War, Vol. I, II, and III. (Chapters by Pospelov, Grechko, A.A., Sokolovski, V.D., Zakharov, M.W., Bagramin, I.K.) Voienizdat, Moscow.

Rendulic, E. (Generaloberst) (1947) The Effect of Extreme Cold on Weapons Wheeled and Track Vehicles. U.S. Army European Command Headquarters, Office of the Chief Historian, Ms. No. D-635.

Rendulic, L. (Gen.) (1947) Combat in Deep Snow. U.S. Army European Command Headquarters, Office of the Chief Historian, Ms. D-106.

Richter, G.D. (ed.) (1960) Geografia Snezhnogo Pokrova (Snow Cover Geography). USSR Academy of Science, Moscow.

Rumiantsev, N.M. (Col.) (1963) Razgrom Vraga v Zapolarii (The destruction of the enemy beyond the polar circle). Voienizdat, Moscow.

Sabaliauskas, V. (Maj.) (1971) Zimniaia ataka (Winter attack). Voiennyi Vestnik. (periodical), No. 2, February.

Sander, K.J. (1959) Tarnen von Feldbefestignugen im Winter (Camouflage of Field Fortifications in Winter). Wehrausbildung in Wort und Bild (periodical) No. 2 (12).

Scott, W.F. (Col.) (1977) Select Soviet Military Writings. U.S. Air Force Transl., U.S. Government Printing Office.

Schaefer, D. (1973) Construction of Field Fortifications with Snow. U.S. Army Cold Regions Research and Engineering Laboratory, Technical Note (unpublished).

Schaefer, D. (1974) Construction and Ballistic Properties of Snow Field Fortifications. U.S. Army Cold Regions Research and Engineering Laboratory, Technical Note (unpublished).

Senger, F. von (1954) Sovietische Kriegslehre (Soviet military doctrine). Ausseupolitik, Vol. 5, No. 3.

Sergeevsky, B.N. (1954) Proshloie Russkoi Semli (The Past of Russian Lands). "Rossika," New York.

Shamshurov, V.K. (Col) (1969) Inzhenernoie Obespetshenie Boyevykh Desitvii Notshiu i v Osobykh Usloviakh (Engineer Troop Combat Support in Night and Special Conditions). Voienizdat, Moscow.

Shapiro, L. (1954) The Army and Party in the Soviet Union. St. Anthony's papers on Soviet Affairs, St. Anthony's College, Oxford.

Sokolov-Strakhov, K.I. (1927) Zimniaia Kampania v Kareii (Winter Campaign in Karelia). Narkomvoienmor, Leningrad.

Sorokin, I. (1939) Osobennosti oborony v zimnikh usloviakh (Special features of winter defense). Voiennyi Vestnik, No. 2, Moscow.

Suomailainen, V. (1949) The battle of Suomussalmi. Military Review, Vol. 19, No. 9.

Swinzow, G.K. (1970a) Methods of Data Acquisition in a Snow Environment. (Explosive Ordnance in Snow). In U.S. Army Cold Regions Research and Engineering Laboratory, Special Report 145.

Swinzow, G.K. (1970b) Fuze Action in Snow. U.S. Army Cold Regions Research and Engineering Laboratory, Special Report 139.

Swinzow, G.K. (1972) Terminal Ballistics in Ordinary Snow. U.S. Army Cold Regions Research and Engineering Laboratory, Technical Report 238.

Topelius, Z. (1883) Times of Battle and Rest. Jansen, McClung and Co., Chicago.

Topelius, Z. (1884) Times of Charles the XII. Jansen, McClung and Co., Chicago.

Vaida, A.P. (1976) War in Ecological Perspective. Plenum, New York.

Vassilieff, M.F. (1955) Winter and war. Cosantoir (periodical) Vol. 15, No. 8, August.

Vladimirtsev, B.A. (1922) The Life of Genghis Khan. Goslitizdat, Moscow.

von Unruh, W. (Gen.) (1947) War Experiences in Russia. U.S. Army Headquarters, Office of the Chief Historian, Ms. No. D-054.

Ward, R.D. (1917) The Weather and the war. Journal of the Military Service Institution of the United States, No. 7.

Werth, A. (1964) Russia at War: 1941-1945. E.P. Dutton & Co., New York.

Yosida, Z. (1958) Physical Studies on Deposited Snow. IV Mechanical Properties. Contributions of the Low Temperature Science Institute, Sapporo, Japan.

Zaionchkovsky (1893) Offensive combat, on the experience of General Skobelev's action in the Battles at Lovtsha, Pleven, and Sheinovo. St. Petersburg, official publication.

Zakharov, M.V. (1967) O Nauchnom Podkhode k Rukovodstvu Voiskami (On Scientific Troop Leadership). Voienizdat, Moscow.

Zeiller, A. (1643) Topographia Sveviae (Swedish Land Description). Matteuas Merian, Printer, Frankfurt. There is also an often quoted Swedish source containing many details about the Battle of Tuttlingen: S. von Puffendorf, (1685). It is in Latin. a 1688 translation title is "Schwedische und Deutsche Kriegsgeschichte." The work is authoritative and covers the Thirty Year War period until the abdication of Queen Christine.

Zhukov, V. (Lt. Col.) (1971) Oborona bataliona zimoi (Battalion defense in winter). Voiennyi Vestnik (periodical), No. 2.

Ziemke, E.F. (1959) The German Northern Theater of Operations, 1940-1945. Department of the Army Pamphlet 20-271.

www.ingramcontent.com/pod-product-compliance
Lightning Source LLC
Chambersburg PA
CBHW080536170426
43195CB00016B/2583